You
too
can
Teach

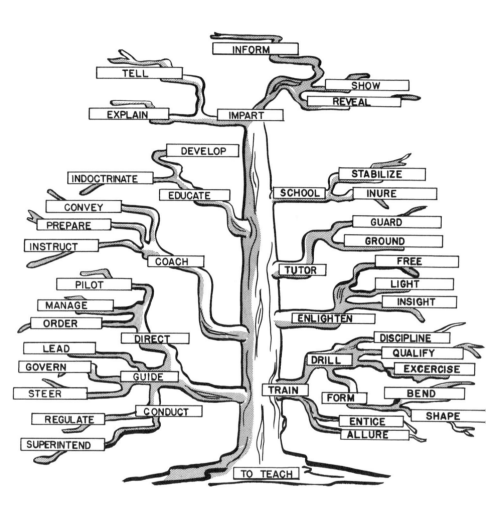

What does teaching mean to you?

You too can Teach

Paul H. Dunn

in collaboration with Cherie B. Parker

Bookcraft

Salt Lake City, Utah

Lithographed in the United States of America
PUBLISHERS PRESS
Salt Lake City, Utah

FOREWORD

"You Too Can Teach" is a book that has been long overdue. Today there are thousands of our members who are being called to serve as teachers in the various organizations of the Church. Most of them are untrained in the art of teaching and all of them are constantly searching for new and more effective ways of reaching their students.

A look at the table of contents will show how extensive the coverage has been on this vital subject of teaching, yet it is all contained in one easy to read volume. Dr. Paul H. Dunn has done a masterful work in outlining and preparing these materials. It is a wealth of information organized to help both trained and untrained teachers to develop a higher level of teaching which will enrich the lives of students everywhere.

In an uncomplicated way, the authors have dealt with the heart of the educational process giving a new focus to concepts, methods and techniques valuable to any teacher. Here is a teachers' manual that is uncomparable in its explanation of educational principles and how they can be utilized. The book gives many practical suggestions on how to deal with common and difficult classroom situations from the primary level to the oldest adult group.

While each subject treated gives definite direction and guidance to the teacher, it leaves him unlimited opportunity for original planning and creativity. Dr. Dunn has focused the reader's attention to one of the fundamental aspects of all teaching, which is that the individual teacher must assume a large share of the responsibility for the classroom climate, the receptivity of students, and the actual learning experience.

The author has had a wide and varied background which qualifies him as a writer in the field of teaching. For several years he played professional baseball. It was during this time that he was called to serve his country in World War II as an infantryman in the "Pacific" for a period of three years. After his return home, he attended several colleges and universities where he earned the Bachelor's, Master's and Doctor's degree. For the past ten years Brother Dunn has been employed by the LDS Department of Education. He served as a seminary teacher and supervisor for four years and for the past six years he has been director of the L.D.S. Institute of Religion at the University of Southern California. Just recently he was appointed Coordinator of Institutes in California, an assignment which makes him responsible for the religious education of over two thousand college students on fifty campuses.

It has been my pleasure to have associated with Dr. Dunn for many years. Having watched him put most of these ideas and concepts into actual practice, I can heartily recommend this book to all dedicated teachers who desire to improve their effectiveness in the classroom.

Dale T. Tingey
Assistant Administrator
LDS Department of Education
Church Unified School System

Publisher's Foreword

Since Dale Tingey's foreword was written, when the book was first published, one of the authors has become a familiar and popular figure to Latter-day Saints. In 1964 Elder Paul H. Dunn was called as a member of the First Council of the Seventy, and since then he has traveled worldwide in the service of the Church. He is well known also for the many books which bear his name.

The Publisher

Dedication

In fond memory of my father
J. HAROLD DUNN
whose life and philosophy were
so characteristic of good teaching

Acknowledgment

The idea for a book of this kind has grown out of needs expressed by many friends and associates and discovered through countless teaching experiences of my own. For the privilege of having these years of teaching opportunities and involvement in church education to begin with, I owe my deepest gratitude to my close friend, Lyman C. Berrett, whose love for the gospel, inspiration and continued encouragement greatly influenced my decision to accept the challenge of teaching youth.

Among the many people who helped directly with this book I am particularly grateful to my wife, Jeanne for her practical suggestions and devotion in helping me see this project through. To Celia Kay Allsop and Noreen Wren for valuable secretarial assistance, and to my Institute colleagues who have acted as sounding boards. To Hal T. Sperry, friend and artist my warmest appreciation for his many illustrative contributions. To Cherie Parker, I owe my special appreciation and thanks for many fine talents and thoughts utilized, for much time and energy spent and dedication given. Because of her years of experience in teaching and her training in Speech and Drama, she is particularly qualified to write Chapter 5, Abstract is my Pink Horse, and Chapter 7, Don't Forget You.

Paul H. Dunn

* * * *

With gratitude to my husband, Edward Myles Parker, whose clear and objective thinking was not only a constant source of encouragement and inspiration, but a safeguard as well. Thanks to Maria Ellsworth, longtime friend and teacher in the field of speech, whose "Word Connotation Tree" gave me the idea which became our frontispiece. And a special thank you to a dear friend, my 81-year-old mentor who read the entire script, and whose uncompromising standards of grammar refused us the luxury of split infinitives and dangling participles.

Finally, and most importantly, I acknowledge a deep debt of gratitude to Dr. Dunn for the opportunity of collaborating with him in the creation of this exciting manuscript. It has been a tremendous and rewarding experience to work with a man of his stature, and on so vital a subject.

Cherie B. Parker

Table of Contents

Thoughts to Inspire

There are obviously two educations. One should teach us how to make a living, and the other how to live.

—James Truslow Adams

Let our teaching be full of ideas. Hitherto it has been stuffed only with facts. . . . The whole art of teaching is only the art of awakening the natural curiosity of young minds for the purpose of satisfying it afterwards.

—Anatole France

The object of teaching a child is to enable him to get along without his teacher.

—Elbert Hubbard

What greater or better gift can we offer the republic than to teach and instruct our youth.

—Cicero

You cannot teach a man anything; you can only help him to find it within himself.

—Galileo

Education means drawing forth from the mind latent powers and developing them, so that in mature years one may apply these powers not merely to success in one's occupation, but to success in the greatest of all arts—the art of living.

—William Lyon Phelps

It is the supreme art of the teacher to awaken joy in creative expression and knowledge.

—Albert Einstein

Those who educate children well are more to be honored than they who produce them; for these only gave them life, those the art of living well.

—Aristotle

If we work upon marble, it will perish; if we work upon brass, time will efface it; if we rear temples, they will crumble into dust; but if we work upon immortal minds, if we imbue them with principles, with the just fear of God and love of our fellowmen, we engrave on those tablets something that will brighten to all eternity.

—Daniel Webster

To know how to suggest is the great art of teaching. To attain it we must be able to guess what will interest; we must learn to reach the childish soul as we might a piece of music. Then, by simple changing of the key, we keep up the attraction and vary the song.

—Amiel

A teacher should, above all things, first induce a desire in the pupil for the acquisition he wishes to impart.

—Horace Mann

Of all the work that is done or that can be done for our country, the greatest is that of educating the body, the mind, and above all the character, giving spiritual and moral training to those who in a few years are themselves to decide the destinies of the nation.

—Theodore Roosevelt

The man who can make hard things easy is the educator.

—Ralph Waldo Emerson

Teach them correct principles and they will govern themselves.

—Joseph Smith

Leading youth to know God, to have faith in his laws, to have confidence in his Fatherhood, and to find solace and peace in his love—this is the greatest privilege of the Church School Teacher.

—David O. McKay

Introduction

TO ALL OF YOU: the clerks, the housewives, the executives, the farmers, who suddenly find yourselves teaching in the Church—Welcome! Welcome to the most frustrating, soul-satisfying service in the world. This book was written for YOU: To help you to understand yourself, your students, your job. Especially the latter in terms of the basic philosophy of education and learning.

We are all teachers. We teach our children, our neighbors, our associates. We are teaching whether we are aware of it or not. The only question is what do we teach and how effectively.

From its inception the Church of Jesus Christ of Latter-day Saints has placed high value upon education. The Lord spoke to His people time after time to remind us of its importance. For instance, such familiar phrases from Church teachings as "The glory of God is intelligence;"[1] "Man cannot be saved by ignorance;"[2] and "Whatever principles of intelligence we attain to in this life, it will rise with us in the resurrection."[3]

As a result, a large portion of the resources and energy of the Church and its people has gone into educational programs. This has been true since the restoration of the Church, and it is given more emphasis year by year.

This was the philosophy which made the school house (which could be used as a chapel as well) the first building to be built whenever Brigham Young called a group of pioneers to found a new settlement. It was the philosophy which built our beautiful Brigham Young University, Ricks College, and the Academy of Juarez; our more than a hundred Institutes of Religion; and organized our thousands of Seminary classes throughout the Church.

---

[1]D&C 93:36
[2]D&C 131:6
[3]D&C 130:18

Yet, the larger burden of teaching still falls upon the lay teacher, not the professional. The lay teacher who cares for the young minds from four to twelve years old in Primary—the teenagers in MIA; and all ages in the Sunday School. The lay teacher is at once both the strength and the weakness of the Church.

Never has the need been greater for clear, effective teaching. Yet among our thousands of lay teachers in the Auxiliairies throughout the Church we find those ranging (in personality and ability) from superior to the lowest levels of inadequacy. We find lessons which have little or no relation to the NEEDS of the students.

The result is that, too often, Church experiences have made little or no impression on the minds and hearts of those who attend. With no impression on the hearts and minds, there can be little impression on the lives of our people. Thus, as has been said, teaching remains the Achilles Heel of any organization.

Since no intelligent parent, teacher, or leader in the Church desires such conditions to exist, it becomes the responsibility of *all* Latter-day Saints to develop themselves and the programs in which they are involved, in order that the quality of learning may always be rich and effective.

At times the question arises as to which age group is most important to be taught. With the clear instructions emphasized over and over by the Lord, the Latter-day Saint can have but one answer: ALL of them!

There are mountains of evidence today that indicate a child is never too young to learn. "Begin with the Child," is the advice from the best psychologists today, just as it was from Christ Himself. Yet, to anyone working with teenagers it is just as obvious that continuing guidance is needed. The adult education movement in this country is powerful evidence that no one is ever too **old** to learn. This is demonstrated over and over as new converts of all ages learn the gospel, learn new habits, and learn a whole new way of life.

Each age has its own problems in learning. Each age must be approached and handled differently. Yet the common denominator for all people of all ages is ROUSE THEIR INTEREST! Rouse their interest and they will be receptive to learning no matter what their age.

The need for teachers in the Church is threefold: First, to train leadership for all the multitudinous tasks of a lay Church; second, to train missionaries to carry out the commandment of the Lord to preach the gospel to every kindred, tongue, and people; and third, we believe that education is an essential element for all members in achieving salvation and exaltation. With this threefold objective, and the firm belief that we learn (and therefore must be taught) from the cradle to the grave, the Latter-day Saint faces a lifelong challenge. The authors hope to aid you in two ways to meet this challenge: (1) By helping you to understand the human nature with which you must constantly contend, so that you can work with it instead of against it. Work with it as the diamond cutter works with the laws of nature, using the law to "cut" the stone for him with a quick blow in exactly the right place. And, (2) by aiding you in developing and using more effective methods and techniques of teaching.

It has been written that "He that governs well leads the blind, but he that teaches gives them eyes."[4] This is at once the basic philosophy of the authors and the purpose of this book. Remembering that the "worth of souls is great in the sight of the Lord" it becomes the personal responsibility of all parents and teachers to give (their) children and students the "eyes" which they need to work out their own salvation.

This book is meant to be read and used as a reference by all teachers in all Auxiliaries and Priesthood Quorums throughout the Church. It is meant as enrichment material for all those engaged in the training of teachers, in the Church. It is meant as a useful tool in the hands of every Bishop,

---

[4]McKay, David O, *Ideals for Living*, P. 139.

every parent, every Priesthood leader. In short, it is meant to be used by anyone, anywhere, who feels the need to be a better teacher.

To that end we offer it humbly, and in the name of Him who called us *all* to be teachers.

Paul H. Dunn

CHAPTER I
Teachers Are Made

"Oh, he's a natural born teacher," is often said of the person who seems particularly successful in the classroom. While it is true that some people have developed personalities which make them more adept at teaching, all of us CAN BECOME effective teachers: For teachers are not often born, *"they are made."* They are made by their learning enough of the basic principles of education to understand the ingredients that make a teacher effective, and coming to some understanding of human nature. The forthcoming chapters deal,

Fig. 2   *Learn the Ingredients of Good Teaching*

primarily, with these ingredients and how to attain them. But before considering them, let us clarify some points of confusion about teaching, the teacher, his attitude, and his job.

WHAT TEACHING IS NOT

Teaching is not so simple as imparting facts or knowledge. As you study the Word Connotation Tree (frontpiece) you will find that "impart" and its synonyms form only one of eight major limbs on the tree "to teach." Imparting does have a place. We do need to memorize some facts, such as dates, places et cetera in Church history. However, facts are important only when they give meaning to concepts or principles. For example, if the knowledge of Brigham Young's courage in surmounting the terrible odds of leading the Saints to a new land in the west, gives a student the urge to surmount a problem which he faces, then the facts of Brigham Young's pilgrimage are important, and the teaching of those facts can be effective. But *imparting* facts is not as important as raising a thirst for facts, stimulating students to think and seek out knowledge and solutions to problems for themselves. As William Lyons Phelps puts it: "The business of a teacher is not to supply information; it is to raise a thirst." Sending a student to search the scriptures for facts is not nearly so effective as sending him to the scriptures to search for the solution to his problem. Getting the facts will be a natural result of his search for a solution; but only in very rare instances will he, on a search for facts, relate his problem to those facts and see the solution therein.

Neither is teaching so simple as meeting daily or weekly with a class, or holding the attention of a class. The teacher of a class of teenagers was heard to remark, "Oh, I'm not really a teacher, I'm a glorified babysitter. I'm there regularly, and if I can keep them from causing a disturbance until the bell rings, what more can they expect?" Certainly such a "teacher" has little conception of what teaching really means. And, fortunately for the Church and for our youth, this type is an exception.

WHAT TEACHING IS

Real teaching causes a change for the better in the behavior of the students as individuals and as a group. For instance, is there less criticism, or more courtesy toward other members of the class? Is there more kindness to the elderly or to the helpless? If there is a non-tithe payer in the group who begins to pay his tithing then real teaching has taken place. If a student overcomes a bad habit and begins to live according to the gospel pattern, then this teacher has brought an understanding of a principle to that person; or his example has given the student courage and the desire to try. For real teaching takes knowledge and understanding out of the books and puts it into the life of the individual. This is necessarily true of the gospel teacher, for as long as the gospel stays in the scriptures with no application to life's problems, there will be no motivation for growth and progress. Gospel teachers must be aware constantly that, regardless of what their current subject may be, their basic objective remains to help their students toward eternal life through the solving of immediate problems with gospel truths.

IMPORTANCE OF TEACHING

Surveys, conducted by the author through the years, have shown that during our young people's most formative years (12 to 18), our programs lose approximately 50% of them from activity in the Church. It shapes up something like this:

Let's say that we start with 10 three-year old youngsters in Junior Sunday School or Primary. Except for moves from the area etc., we will have the same 10 youngsters when they are 12 years of age. But between 12 and 14 years we lose one of the 10. From 14 to 16 years we lose 2 more, leaving 7 out of 10. Then from 16 to 18 years we lose another 2, leaving only 50% of our original 10. Any improvement in that ratio in a given class is directly traceable to the teacher. For whether the Church retains that 50% or the potential 100%, it is mostly in the hands of the teachers, that is, in what the lay teachers are doing both in and out of their classes.

Therefore, to the individual class member, the importance of good teaching can scarcely be exaggerated. In every class he attends he *will learn something!* Will it be living gospel truths, presented in a positive manner by a carefully, prayerfully prepared teacher? Or will it be such secondary learning

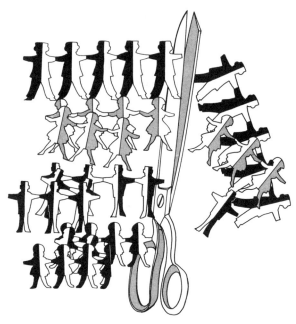

Fig. 3

How Effective is our Teaching

as "Church teachers are dopes, they don't know what they're talking about." "They say one thing and do another." "If we make enough rumpus the teacher will leave and we can sneak out." "If we pretend we've read the lesson and don't understand it, he'll give us the answers anyway." All these are typical remarks made by young people about Church classes. It is obvious that the teacher is the only one who can change these remarks for the better.

However, the effect does not end with the individual. How does the teaching that called forth those remarks effect the home and the Church? It results in a new generation of parents and leaders who are weak in the faith; less committed to gospel way of life; with insufficient growth and development to carry the burden of parenthood, and to spread the gospel according to the Lord's plan for these latter days.

It means the same weakness in the community and society as a whole. Weak teaching of gospel truths breeds weak citizens; citizens ill-equipped to build; citizens susceptible to the welfare state, Communism, and all the other "isms" with which the tyrants and dictators seek to take over the minds of men and wipe out their free agency. The strength of the nation, the community, and the Church comes only from the strength of the individual members. Therefore, teaching the basic truths of the gospel remains of prime importance to our future, and the future of the world. For only with those truths on which to build, will the individual gain the personal strength, the internal security, and the knowledge necessary to gain eternal life. We must never forget that the future leaders of both Church and our land are sitting in our classes *today*.

Fig. 4

Future Leaders Sit in our Classes Today

YOUR CALLING AS A TEACHER

All this makes the role of the teacher one of the most important in the world—with an appalling burden of responsibility. Yet we say to you, do not be frightened by it. Grasp the challenge and opportunity it affords you with both hands, for YOU TOO, CAN TEACH! We do wish to impress you with the responsibility which is yours. As Asahel Woodruff says, "Teaching assignments must be taken seriously. . . . A full committment to the gospel and the assignment is essential. No half-way acceptance of the task will do."[1] But once you are committed, we will try to show you how well YOU CAN carry out your teaching assignment.

Two other responsibilities of a teacher should be considered: The continuing need to search for more gospel knowledge; and the continuing need to live so as to be a source of inspiration to your students. Woodruff devotes a whole chapter to the premise that teachers must *become* gospel scholars. Among other things, he points out that the words of a teacher have greater potential for good and greater potential for harm than the words of most other people. It is imperative that we teach *truth*. Neither our ideas nor our interpretations, but truth as it is found in the Four Standard Works of the Church, and as it comes from the living Prophet today.

There is an old English prayer by Donne which says in part: "Wilt Thou forgive that sinne by which I have led other to Sinne? And made my sinne their door?" This most surely applies to our words as well as to our actions; for we cannot stop the effects of our words on the lives of the people whom we lead to believe a half-truth or a wrongly interpreted truth.

We can seldom know how much our actions will influence the life of another. While it is true that we cannot *give* our testimonies to our students, we are the pace-setters for them to develop their own. Our convictions, as shown by our lives, can be such a source of inspiration that our students' faith and testimonies will grow and be strengthened. Can you teach honesty with words when your students know you are considered a "sharp" business man? Will your eloquent plea for integrity affect the life of a boy who knows you habitually exceed the speed limit and break other traffic regulations in your driving? What will integrity come to mean to him if you criticize the Bishop or other Authorities of the Church? Will such actions on your part strengthen their faith and testimonies? Since no one can hope to reach the Celestial Kingdom

---

[1]Woodruff, Asahel, Teaching the Gospel, Chap. I; Deseret Sunday School Union Board.

without faith and a testimony, it becomes the responsibility of teachers to do all they can to inspire students to work and seek for both. Living the gospel ourselves will give them the greatest inspiration possible.

DEVELOPING A POINT OF VIEW

Each teacher must develop his own philosophy, his own point of view if he is to reach anything near his potential.

Fig. 5

Build a Philosophy of Education

This too, is part of "making" a teacher. The group of quotations found in the front of the book has influenced the thinking of the authors and helped them to develop a philosophy. As you study and work and read, you will find that you, too, will begin to form a personal point of view. Study the Word Connotation Tree (frontpiece) to see the many sides of teaching, then develop a philosophy of education which will include the most important areas. As an example, if you have thought of a teacher only as a guide, your study of the branches on that "limb" may lead you to shift your aim to the limb called "enlighten," whose branches are more in harmony with gospel teaching ideas.

If you are not sure of your philosophy of teaching or of the characteristics you'd like to develop, study this list on the teaching personality of Jesus, the Master Teacher:

1. He was friendly and had an extremely approachable manner. All classes sought him out to have as a dinner guest or as a counsellor.

2. His well-balanced, integrated personality exerted tremendous influence upon all who met Him. He possessed great poise and natural dignity.

3. He was tender and kind to the weak. He truly loved people even when He hated what they did.

4. He had tremendous vigor and power in expressing Himself. It was said that He spoke with power and authority, not like the scribes.

5. His courageous struggles against His enemies and His bold facing of a horrible death, made the things He said even more effective.

6. He embodied all of the high and lofty teachings with which He inculcated His hearers.

7. His faith and prayers, His trust in the Father were examples far more powerful than all that He *said* about prayer and faith.

8. He was a blend of the physical and the spiritual: He loved the world and its life and activities, yet His spirituality was always supreme.

CONSIDER YOUR OWN PERSONALITY

Strive constantly to improve your teaching personality, methods, and techniques. Together with the above list, study this group of traits, and so forth which the teenager expects of a teacher. Couched in the words of the teenager, it too, will be a valuable guide. It is the result of some five years of surveys made by the author through Institute, Seminary, and Auxiliary classes of several widely different Stakes in Southern California. The results were compiled in the order of their importance as indicated by the students.

What the Teenager Expects of a Teacher

1. Dress like regular teachers, not like cheer-leaders, sweater-girls or bobby-soxers.
2. Act like adults all the time. Don't mimic us or speak down to us.
3. We don't like to be ridiculed or embarrassed. Don't be sarcastic.

Fig. 6

Control Yourself

4. *Control Yourself.* It is silly to "blow your top" in front of us.
5. Speak so everyone can hear. Don't talk so fast we can't follow, or so slow we get bored.
6. Treat all of us fair and square, NO favorites.
7. Don't pick on us for every little thing that happens.
8. Have good suggestions for things to do instead of a lot of "don'ts" (Positive teaching)

9. Remember that we have feelings, so try to understand when we are not up to par. Please don't "bawl us out" in front of others.

10. Don't brag about your life and background, like what you always did in college or high school.

11. Don't run down our Ward or Stake by making nasty remarks about it, or comparing it unfavorably with others in the Church.

12. "Know your stuff" in teaching and know what you are going to do each Sunday (or day).

13. Have something for us to do each class period. We don't like to just sit and listen all the time. And we don't like the same old thing every day.

14. Talk over what is to be done instead of starting right in before we know what to do. We can't discuss something when we don't know what it's all about.

15. Don't go over our heads. Ask clear questions. Use words we understand. Explain directions and assignments so we know what to do.

16. Give us a chance to answer questions and give our ideas. Don't have all the answers yourself. Don't repeat all the points made in discussion.

Interestingly enough the above list is almost identical (though differently worded) with a similar list taken from 12,000 letters received on a composition entitled "The Teacher Who Has Helped Me Most." The writing of these compositions was the result of a Quiz Kids program which gave a scholarship to the teacher most convincingly described. The letters came from students in Grades 8-12 all over the United States.

A Western educator, Frank Hart, made a similar survey of 10,000 high school seniors. The students were asked to think of the teacher they liked most and the one they liked least and to write the reasons for their choices. The results were much like those of the other two surveys mentioned. Mr. Hart comments on the reasons given as follows: "One can scarcely fail to be profoundly impressed if not actually amazed, by the keen, searching analysis, the mature critical judgment, the exacting standards, the high purpose, and the idealism of the high school senior."

By way of summary, Paul A. Witty, a Professor of Education, is quoted as saying:

"The above reactions—typical of the thousands made —show the significance of a mental hygienic approach in the classroom. In fact, this emphasis is the outstanding feature of the letters.

"These boys and girls appear to be grateful to the school in proportion to the degree that it offers security, individual success, shared experience and opportunities for personal and social adjustments. And these are precisely the factors which promote good learning."

ATTITUDE IN TEACHING

Of equal importance with some understanding of human nature and the need for gospel scholarship is the attitude with which the teacher approaches his assignment. His attitude is contagious. It is equally contagious whether it is enthusiastic or negative. Therefore, he will set his own stage. In Les Giblin's book, *How to Have Power and Confidence in Dealing With People*, he says in Chapter 4:

"Whether you realize it or not, you control the actions and attitudes of others by your own actions and attitudes. Your own attitudes are reflected back to you from the other person almost as if you stood before a mirror. Act or feel hostile and the other fellow reflects this hostility back to you. Shout at him and he is almost compelled to shout back. Act calmly and unemotionally and you turn away his anger before it gets started. Act enthusiastic and you arouse the enthusiasm of the other person. Act confidently and the other person has confidence in you. . . . Don't mumble your words as if you were afraid to express them. Speak out. Watch your posture. A slumped figure signifies that you find the burdens of life too heavy for you to bear. A drooping head signifies you are defeated by life. Hold your head up. Straighten your shoulders. Walk with a confident step, as if you had somewhere important to go.

Walk . . . as if you had somewhere important to go, as indeed you have. Walk with purpose, having worked out your objectives, both general and specific. Walk with courtesy toward your students and fellow workers. Walk with friendliness, that no student will fear to approach you with his problems. Walk with confidence, knowing you have done all that you can to prepare, and can safely leave yourself in the hands of the Lord. Walk with humbleness, having asked the Lord to walk with you."

THE TASK BEFORE US

Many will be the problems you face in finding methods, keeping discipline and so forth. Teaching is a complex task, for no two classes or groups are alike. A fine method worked out for one may be useless for the next. (But do not destroy any notes or material you have worked up, for you will re-use most of it in one manner or another.)

Fig. 7   *Survey Your Class*

Begin by surveying your class. Try to determine what strength and what weakness each student brings to the class. Then start to tailor your approach, your philosophy, your illustrations et cetera, to fit the needs of this particular group. For example if you were shifted from Kanab, Utah, to Los Angeles or New York, would you expect to use the same approach, the same illustrations? If you were given the same age group, you would be teaching exactly the same material in all three places. The same would be true of Japan, Australia, Great Britain, or South America, as well. However, in Japan for instance, you would need to remember that your students would come, not only from a different culture, they might not even be familiar with Christianity except as they had absorbed it in a few short months. Would you be able to use the same illustrations from American customs or history? You might; it would depend on the age and education of the members of the class.

We need to realize fully that the Church is now world wide, yet it is ONE Church. The lesson material will continue to come from one source only: The General Boards in Salt Lake City, Utah. Teachers all over the world teach the same gospel from the same source to any given age group. Yet each teacher must adapt that material to the best use of HIS students. Use that manual or textbook as the guide to keep your feet planted firmly on the path. Then with your eyes on the goal, as laid out by the Church, reach that goal in the way most effective for your students. But, as one MIA Conference speaker said, "Remember that if the goal is to build a house, then ALL of you must end up with a *house*."

One of the most prevalent problems in teaching is becoming stereotyped, getting in a rut, developing one method only. Nearly all teachers have a favorite method of teaching, one technique in which they are most adept. But we need to remember that "a rut is just a grave with open ends," and one of the best ways to kill a class is for the teacher to get buried in a one-method rut. In the chapter on techniques will be found many suggested variations from which you can choose procedures. It is essential that you develop adeptness in more than one.

The most common problems brought to those in a supervisory capacity are, what methods can I use, and how can I keep discipline while learning takes place? In the forthcoming chapters we hope to give you many practical answers to both problems.

NOW THAT YOU ARE AWARE

Now that you are aware of some of the areas of concern that a teacher must face and the seemingly appalling responsibility he must assume—Let's Begin! Let's begin to find out, specifically, how to meet problems, and how to discharge this teaching responsibility with love and understanding. Let us prove to you that

YOU TOO, CAN TEACH!

POINTS TO REMEMBER:

1. Teachers are MADE, by learning the ingredients that make them effective and by coming to some understanding of human nature.
2. Teaching is not so simple as imparting facts or meeting regulary with a group.
3. Real teaching is taking truth out of the books and putting it into the lives of students so that their behavior may be changed for the better.
4. Good teaching is of prime importance to the individual, the home, the community, and the Church. Poor teaching weakens them all.
5. The role of the teacher calls for continuing improvement in gospel scholarship and gospel living.
6. The teaching personality of Jesus gives us the best pattern.
7. The teacher's attitude will be reflected in the attitudes of the class members.
8. Survey your group and tailor your approach, illustrations, etc., to its particular needs.
9. Your manual or lesson material is the guide to keep you on the path as you adapt the material to the needs of your group.
10. Vary your methods and techniques to better keep the interest of your class.

CHAPTER II

Understanding Those We Teach

PART I

Exploring Their Differences

During World War II, the writer was serving in the South Pacific and on one occasion he came upon a wounded enemy soldier trapped in a cave. Though the soldier was near death, he made every effort to defend himself. But in his weakened condition it was impossible to resist for long and he surrendered. Since the two of us represented different governments, cultures, and basic philosophies of life, it was natural for him to withdraw into himself. He even tried to hide his face behind his arms. Though I could not speak his language, it was obvious that he was afraid of the unexpected. It took me several minutes to convince him that I really was trying to offer him help.

After cleaning out his wound and giving him food and water, I found one of our interpreters and asked him to assist me in communicating with this young soldier. To our amazement, we found that we had much in common. He too, had been drafted by his country and sent to fight and kill. He had been away from his home for several years and did not know his family's whereabouts, and he was much concerned for their welfare. He too, was very homesick. He had left high school and was engaged to be married when his country called. He wanted very much to go home to a happy peaceful world. The more we talked the more alike we found ourselves to be, even to the idolizing of the same American baseball stars. In fact, had the decision to continue fighting World War II been ours to make, we would have quickly shaken hands and hurried home.

KNOWLEDGE BRINGS UNDERSTANDING

This experience taught me a basic lesson in human nature; Once we understand each other's feelings, purposes, and ways of life, it is possible to become friends. And so I have found it to be in teaching, for we are working with people, not subjects. The individual should be the center of every lesson taught. The individual reacts only according to HIS past experiences, and interprets things in the light of HIS experiences. Therefore, the successful teacher will make every effort to understand the individual and become his friend. Then he can use the trust engendered by that friendship, and the discoveries he has made, to "bring home" the subject matter in the manner most needed by the student.

Every student, young or old, brings to class factors from his heritage and environment which make him an individual. Everyone accepts the fact that no two people are exactly alike in respect to attributes, physical, mental, emotional, or spiritual. Bolton, in his *Everyday Psychology for Teachers*, puts it this way:

"It is not difficult to discover abundant cases of individual variations. There are the giants and dwarfs, the tall and the short, the blondes and brunettes, the beautiful and ugly, black and white, good and bad, choleric and phlegmatic, brilliant and stupid, blue-eyed and brown-eyed, and other extremes too numerous to chronicle. Between these extremes there are all shades of apparent differences. Between these obvious differences there are innumerable variations which are not so apparent and hence thought not to exist. Some persons burst forth into song with the most meager training while others, with the best master, can never carry a tune or discover discord; some are ready spellers, while others are hopeless; some are born mathematicians, while others are never able to progress beyond the merest rudiments. One child clearly exhibits mechanical genius, while another can never learn to put together the simplest contrivance; one can memorize verbatim with the greatest ease, while another can never repeat a quotation; one person picks up the pen and, without training, begins to produce literature, while another cannot chronicle accurately the simplest event; one mounts the platform and charms the multitude with his eloquence, while another is made mute in the presence of an audience."[1]

THE VARIETY WITHIN A SINGLE CLASS

What many lay teachers do not realize is that there are many of these individual differences in existence within a single class. For example, in the average Church class of twenty students, regardless of age these individual differences can be found to challenge the teacher:

Fig. 8   *What a Student Brings to Class*

1. Physical characteristics, including handicaps
2. Emotional maturity
3. Chronological age

---

[1]Bolton, F. E., *Everday Psychology for Teachers,* Charles Scribner's Son, New York, 1923.

4. Mental ability, quickness, alertness, capacity
5. State of health
6. Sex (male and female needs often differ)
7. Family background
8. Marital status
9. Church experience
10. Basic formal education
11. Special aptitudes and skills
12. Life ambitions and goals

Any one, or a combination of the above differences, will tend to affect an individual's ability to learn. (This will be discussed in Part 2 of this chapter.) We find that the ability and capacity to learn are directly related to the interests of the individual, and by that which motivates him. Therefore, it is imperative that the teacher be aware of these many differences that exist in his class. He must recognize and respond to these differences if he is to hold the interest and obtain the desired participation of his students.

A CASE IN POINT

Marshall and Roger are in the same Sunday School class which is studying Church History. The lesson is on the pioneers. Marshall's parents are fourth generation Mormons, whose ancestors left Nauvoo and helped to settle Salt Lake Valley. His family has a Book of Remembrance with pictures and pages from old diaries that help him to know about his heritage. On the other hand, Roger's mother is a recent convert and his father a non-member. A teacher who has an understanding of the background of these two boys, will avoid embarrassing or discouraging Roger, while at the same time he will utilize Marshall's knowledge to the benefit of the entire class. Without knowledge of the background it would be seemingly obvious that Roger was ignorant and probably stupid.

ANOTHER CASE

Betty and Carol are teenagers in the same grade at school. Betty's parents are college graduates. They take an active interest in reading, the cultural arts, current events, and community activities. They take Betty to operas, concerts, art exhibits, museums and dramatic productions. They have a fairly adequate library in their home, subscribe to several good magazines, and Betty has her own set of classics to read. On the other hand Carol's parents finished high school, but went to work instead of college. They have no interest in books, and participate in no community events or cultural activities. Carol spends her spare time watching television of her own choosing, and reading comic books. She has never seen a legitimate play or been to a concert.

The teacher who is unaware of the differences in the backgrounds of these two girls, could easily label Betty as more intelligent than Carol. She could even conclude that Carol was stupid, which might not be the case at all. She simply may have been unguided, having had no opportunity to use a potentially good mind.

These two illustrations are not extreme cases, since such differences can be found in the typical Church classroom. Because this is true, the teacher must start his lesson preparation from the level of the student with the least background in the subject, and to know what that level is. For the dedicated teacher will make it part of his assignment to learn the various backgrounds, the strengths and weaknesses, of his students and use this information in his teaching. It seems obvious that the teacher who remains unaware of the individual differences among his students, will make many mistakes in the teaching process. In so doing, he will deprive his students of as many opportunities to learn.

WAYS OF LEARNING INDIVIDUAL DIFFERENCES

From the front of the classroom most students look alike. That is, it is difficult to tell by *looking* at an individual, what his ambitions are, his basic mental capacity, or from what kind of family he comes. Many times our quick observations are not sufficient to give us the necessary inventory of facts to understand an individual's makeup. But there are many ways the teacher can obtain the information he needs to be effective in working with the class.

One of the best and easiest is to design and duplicate a simple interest questionaire that can be completed by each member of the class. This information will provide a useful background on each student. (See sample, Figure 9).

NAME

FATHER'S OCCUPATION

HOW LONG HAVE YOU LIVED IN THIS AREA?

NUMBER OF BROTHERS?

SISTERS?

SCHOOL SUBJECTS LIKED BEST?

SPORTS YOU LIKE

SCHOLASTIC PLANS

CHURCH JOBS HELD

Fig. 9

Develop a Student Interest Inventory

Such questions as, What is your father's name, your mother's and their occupation? How long have you lived in this city? This state? How many brothers and sisters do you have, and what are their ages? Do you have any health problems? What school subjects do you like best and least, and why? What troubles you most in school? What are your plans after school? When you have free time what do you like to do? Name the sports you like to watch, and those in which you like to participate. What is your favorite kind of music? What is the number of hours spent each week watching TV? What are your favorite TV and radio programs? What kind of stories, books, magazines, etc., do you like to read? List your favorite kind of motion pictures. What outside work do you do? To what organizations do you belong? Etc. etc.

Obviously, the teacher should gear his questions to the age-group involved, making necessary variations for the very young or the adult groups. For the youngsters who do not read or write, the questionaire could be sent home by the child, to be filled out by the parents and brought back to the next class by the child. There are many variations of this questionaire, use your own judgment and imagination as to what will give you the most useful information.

KEEP IT CONFIDENTIAL

It is imperative that information collected by such questionaires be kept confidential and in a safe place. A card file or looseleaf notebook serves the purpose well in keeping the information close at hand where it can be kept up-to-date. It has been my experience that many times a class member who seemed bored or unable to be reached in the usual class activity, could be brought into active participation by gearing a particular point in the lesson to his interest area as shown by his background.

OTHER AIDS TO UNDERSTAND

Having students write brief biographies, or compositions within their range and experience, are two other ways of obtaining valuable information about them. Again the teacher needs to keep in mind the age and experience of his students. But it is remarkable how much insight can be gained by having class members write a one or two page history of their lives, giving the highlights and unusual experiences. The events they consider as highlights can give a teacher much understanding of his student.

Many times, especially with older groups, teachers find it difficult to stimulate interest in a particular subject because it is the same subject studied by the class time and time again. For instance, it is not uncommon for the New Testament to be taught to college age or adult groups four or five times in as many years. It may not be the same manual, or written by the same author, but as far as the class is concerned it is still the same subject. For teachers who find themselves facing this problem, it would be well to find out at the beginning of the year which students do have a good foundation in the subject, and which do not.

This can be determined quite easily by having them write a composition on different parts of the manual (perhaps using the chapter headings, etc.) Another is by creating a knowledge inventory (Check list) on the material to be covered during the year. Often we all have the idea that we know more than we do about a given topic. A simple true or false quiz, or a sentence completion test, will show the students that they still have more to learn. (See Chapter XI for illustrations). Information gained from such quizzes would be extremely helpful to the teacher in preparing his lessons. It would enable him to put the emphasis of any lesson where there is a weakness in the knowledge of the students. In the case of a student who has very little knowledge on the topic (such as Roger in the Church History class), he might be given special reading assignments and/or brief reports to be brought to class. This would tend to bring him to the level of the rest of the class much faster. On the other hand, the extra knowledge of some of the students could be utilized more effectively, thus adding interest and strength to the class. Intelligent handling of the problems of individual differences can be the key to successful teaching, as these problems can be either stumbling blocks or stepping stones to learning.

BEING SENSITIVE TO NAMES

Even so small a thing as a student's name can become a factor in successful or unsuccessful teaching. To a student, his name is the sweetest sound in the entire language. When a teacher remembers it, whether there be twenty or a hundred in the class, the student will glow with inner pleasure and pride. The teacher's pronunciation of his name, correctly, distinctly, and RESPECTFULLY, can take on an aspect of major importance in the mind of an individual student. Many people have names that are forever the butt of jokes and ridicule. (Miss Picklesimer comes to mind.) But if the teacher shows, by his handling of the name, that he considers it as good or as important as any other name in the

Fig. 10

group, then the other students will take their cue from him and act accordingly.

THE CASE OF TERRY
WHO-CAME-FOR-SOMETHING-TO-DO

Another problem, which offers unusual opportunities to the teacher, is the boy or girl who is a non-member of the Church. Often these non-members are enticed by the seemingly endless fun and activity shared by the L.D.S. young people. Most frequently they come to either MIA or Primary first, but they can be found in almost any class in the Church. Let me tell you about Terry.

He was a boy who came with an L.D.S. friend. Terry did not belong to any church, his parents had never taught him to pray or to read the scriptures. His home was spiritually empty. His parents prided themselves on being "intellectuals" who had a grasp of psychology and science, and felt no need for religion. Terry came to church with his friend because he was bored. He was bored at home on Sundays because his father spent most of his time watching TV, mowing the lawn, or washing the car; while his mother cooked and cleaned house.

When Terry was invited to come to Church he accepted it as "something to do." In order for the teacher to reach the heart of this boy, he had to abandon the traditional Church approach and put himself in Terry's position. He had to project himself into the feelings of the boy and empathize with him. Empathy demands the imagination and ability to live someone else's life with him, or as the Old Indian put it, "walk in his moccasins." The teacher succeeded in influencing Terry because he sincerely desired to do so. His desire was deep enough to make him go out of his way to talk with the boy after class, and to encourage him to read selected articles which would stimulate his interest. But he was careful not to destroy completely the doubt about spiritual matters with which he had been reared, until he could find something with which to replace it. For when a teacher helps to take away an undesirable quality, one even more undesirable may replace it.

Fig. 11   *Replace an Old Habit with a New One*

"Nature abhors a vacuum" is a well-understood scientific axiom, and it is as true in working with the characteristics of people as it is in the laboratory. If we want to break a bad habit, the best way is to replace it with a good one. In this case, the teacher led Terry, little by little, to know Jesus Christ; first as an historical figure, a carpenter who was strong and who could walk many miles in a day and sleep out of doors. This Terry could understand and appreciate. Then, gradually, the teacher led him into the moral teachings of Jesus. This the boy could accept also. Whether he would ever be able to accept Jesus Christ as the Saviour of the World, would depend entirely on how much he could learn to accept and trust his teacher. This, in turn, would depend on the teacher's understanding of Terry, and his acceptance of those qualities brought from Terry's home environment, qualities which made him different from every boy in the class.

DIFFERENCES ARE NOT THE WHOLE PICTURE

In spite of all the differences we have discussed, man shares his basic NEEDS with all men. Each of us has the same need for food and water, for air to breathe and sleep to rest our bodies. Aside from these physiological needs, we share the same need to be accepted by the group, to be a creative part of the world, to have a measure of self-esteem, and some sense of purpose for living.

PART 2

Understanding the Whole Student and How He Learns

"I wish I could understand my students. WHY do they do the things they do? Why do they act THAT way?" These are the comments of conscientious teachers everywhere. We hear them frequently—for it is the goal of the conscientious teacher to understand, as far as possible, the individuality of each of his students. If learning is to take place, it is vitally important that the teacher does come to know and understand those whom he teaches.

Modern science, as applied to education, has helped us to know much about people—how they grow, how they learn, how they adjust. As this type of knowledge has been extended, it has seemed to underline the importance of understanding the student. However, until recently, education tended to concern itself with particular aspects of the individual, rather than the *whole person*. As Olson and Hughes point out in their book on the growth of the child:

> "The child was sent to school to be taught subject matter and to church to be taught religion. And it was assumed that the patterns of emotional behavior would be developed in some intangible way in the interactions between parents and their children in the home. However, this type of thinking is giving way to a much more integrated approach in which it is recognized that, although the child may be observed from the standpoint of various facets of behavior, he functions as a total personality which should be thought of as such."[2]

As we said, there is much we do know about how the individual grows and develops. We have discussed the many differences he brings to class and how to utilize them in

---

[2]W. C. Olson and B. O. Hughes, *Growth of the Child as a Whole.* McGraw-Hill, 1943.

teaching. Now let us consider the nature of the student, that we may discuss more intelligently some methods and techniques of teaching that will both permit and encourage learning.

EACH INDIVIDUAL IS REALLY FIVE

One of the fascinating things we have learned about human beings is that each one is really five: He is physical, intellectual, emotional, social, and spiritual. In order to understand the

Fig. 12   *Each Person is Really "Five"*

behavior and the needs of an individual, it is necessary to understand that all of these forces are at work within him all of the time. We must consider the WHOLE person before attempting to deal with any problems with which he may be confronted.

This fundamental truth can be stated as the following three basic principles of human development, the knowledge of which will aid us in understanding the whole man:

    1. Each individual grows and behaves as a total organism. Therefore we must consider all aspects of his makeup as a person.

2. Growth, development, and behavior changes are continuous and uneven.
3. Behavior, even a single act, is complex and grows out of many complex causes.

With these three principles in mind, let us discuss the five sides of man.

THE PHYSICAL SIDE

Even in the same family no two individuals are exactly alike physically—with the possible exception of identical twins.

Fig. 13   *No Two Individuals are Exactly Alike*

Each is likely to be advanced in some ways, retarded in others. Neither is there any rule governing the length of time an individual will remain in any one stage of development. Sometimes one boy will shoot up suddenly, attaining in a single year the growth another boy of the same age will take several years to achieve.

Many teachers accommodate almost automatically for these obvious differences in size; but tend to overlook the emotional, intellectual, social and spiritual effects of such differences. All of these are significant because they affect the way an individual responds, and the way he sees himself. It is not unusual for the teacher of a pre-teen or teenage group to assign to a physically mature student a mental or emotional maturity that that student has not yet achieved. This too, affects the attitudes and behavior of students toward learning and toward each other. The teacher's actions toward individual students can cause an emotional disturbance in both the individual and the group.

It may be nothing more than the teacher looking at that boy or girl more frequently as he talks to the group. As simple a thing as that can give rise to the "teacher's pet" idea in a class, causing resentment toward both the teacher and that student. Once such an idea starts it takes very little to feed it. Few things can make a boy or girl more miserable than to be tagged with some such misnomer and to be ostracized because of it.

Again, unconsciously feeling the big boy is more mature, the teacher may give him a responsibility or assignment of which he is not yet capable. In other words, the teacher will expect too much of him. This works in reverse as well: the boy or girl who is smaller in stature than the group is often treated like a child by the teacher. The small boy is apt to feel he must be more belligerent, and the small girl to act more bored or sexy just to be sure everyone will know they are as "old" as the group. Always we come back to the need for understanding the individual student. Know him and love him so that you can help him to cope with the emotions caused by being "different" from the group in any way.

There are some other physical problems which directly influence behavior and therefore must be kept in mind. Because these problems are difficult to detect, a student may be held accountable for conduct over which he has no control. It is now known that glandular disorders and certain defects in nutrition will lead students to behave in an abnormal way. Some individuals tend to become overactive, while others will be slow moving, incapable of speeding up or of working hard.

For example, there were two brothers we can call Bill and Jack. Bill was only ten, but was head and shoulders taller than twelve year-old Jack, and thirty pounds heavier. But Bill had a pituitary gland disturbance which had caused the shell of his body to grow faster than his internal processes. He was not weak mentally, but physically an eight year-old could pummel the daylights out of him, and did so regularly. It was heartbreaking to watch the drubbings he took as smaller and more belligerent boys discovered he could not defend himself. They not only drubbed him physically, they called him a coward and treated him with contempt as their own small egos swelled at the thought of beating someone bigger than themselves.

Consider the emotional upheaval of a mentally normal boy, constantly being forced to try to defend himself. As his mother said, his tears were not the result of the physical pain, but rage and despair at his lack of strength. If a teacher did not make the effort to learn this boy's real problem, he might jump to the conclusion that the boy was lazy, cowardly, or just plain ornery.

Such conditions in students can cause the lay teacher, who is unaware of such problems, to make demands and apply pressures that are unnecessary and even harmful to students. As teachers we need to keep foremost in our minds that the manner in which a person grows and develops physically is all important in his attitudes toward learning and to life in general.

THE INTELLECTUAL SIDE

In many ways, the development of an individual's mental processes is similar to the pattern of his physical growth. Studies of the growth of intelligence in human beings indicate a rapid growth in infancy, and continuous development at a gradually diminishing rate until maturity is reached. Other findings reveal that mental ability or capacity to learn is different in each person. While it is true that intelligences do differ in greatness, we believe that all of the children of our Heavenly Father have the ultimate potential to become like

Fig. 14
Mental Capacity to Learn Varies as an Individual Grows

Him. This then, suggests to each teacher that every student in a class is capable of learning. A quotation familiar to Latter-day Saints is found in the Book of Abraham:

"Now the Lord has shown unto me, Abraham, the intelligences that were organized before the world was; and among all these there were many of the noble and great ones. And God saw these souls that they were good, and He stood in the midst of them, and He said: These I will make my rulers; for He stood among those that were spirits, and He saw that they were good; and He said unto me: Abraham, thou art one of them; thou wast chosen before thou was born."[3]

Whether or not learning takes place depends on how much motivation and interest is created for the student by the teacher. Also, we must realize that, because of the differences in their growth stages, the intellect of any group of students may vary from an I.Q. (intelligence quotient) of

[3]Book of Abraham, 3:22-23; *Pearl of Great Price.*

seventy to one hundred and forty. This makes it necessary for the teacher to vary his approach accordingly, always starting his preparation on the level of the least experienced without lowering the quality. (An example is the story of Marshall and Roger in Part I). Then with special assignments and other variations he can maintain the interest of the student with the richer background as well. The class as a whole should be kept at an average learning level, while at the same time the teacher seeks to satisfy all extremes. In other words, let there be something for each student on his own level of learning. Much patience as well as much ingenuity must be exercized with both the slow learner and the very fast, to keep each of them progressing to the best of his ability. As you will find in the chapter on techniques, problem solving is one excellent method of reaching all levels.

Lay teachers need to understand that I.Q.'s are educational *barometers*, they are not stationary at any level, high, low, or average. Measurements of intelligence do assist the educator in understanding the amount of *participation* and *exposure* an individual has had to a variety of specific activities. A point to remember is that the amount of learning experienced by a student in any given area of study, is in direct correlation to the interest and motivation he has in that area.

That is to say, his lack of interest in religion (due to his particular background) may keep his apparently low level of "intelligence" at much less than his actual potential. But if in the process of taking religion out of the books and putting it into his life, you bring him to some understanding of what living gospel principles can add to his well being, you may discover he is far more intelligent than you supposed. The difference would be that you had piqued his interest and motivated him to some positive action in gospel living. We know that the quickest and surest way to prove the truth of any gospel principle is to live it. This is the promise of the Lord. For example, if you want to know if the law of tithing works, try paying it honestly and cheerfully, and you will soon have your answer that it does. The door is unlocked, but you and I must supply the first act of faith by turning the knob to see for ourselves that it will open. If we can show this to our students we can stimulate their interest and motivate them to action in gospel living. The result will be a greatly accelerated learning process in those students.

THE EMOTIONAL SIDE

It has been said that "emotions are the greatest motivating factors in human experience."[4] While there is no complete agreement among psychologists as to the usefulness of true emotional experience in people, there is strong agreement in the field of human behavior that all learning is affected by how an individual "feels"; and that these feelings are closely related to bodily well-being. George Dumas, a noted French authority, has pointed out that:

"Vascular-muscle functions, skeletal-muscle functions, and the regulatory chemical action of the glands of internal secretion are all present in both so-called feeling and emotional behaviour."[5]

In other words, one's whole physical being is involved in emotions. The emotion (caused by the situation) creates a physical reaction which is an actual chemical change in the body. This in turn affects the intellect or mind. For instance, in these days of turmoil and tension, most of us are familiar with so-called nervous indigestion: Fear or anger (emotions) cause a tightening of the stomach muscles (the physical reaction) and the release of an excess of the powerful digestive acids (the chemical change), which in turn results in a dull, sluggish feeling affecting the ability to think clearly. This is the reason doctors tell us not to eat if we are emotionally upset—it creates a chain of reactions throughout our entire bodies.

In a spiritual setting (the Church class) the bad emotion will create a mind-set or mental barrier which will block learning. This might be termed a "mental indigestion," in which case you can feed them all the facts, but they will not absorb any part of them.

---

[4]Paul L. Boynton, *Psychology of Child Development;* Minneapolis Educational Publishers, Inc., 1938.
[5]George Dumas, *Nouveau Traite de Psychologie,* Paris: Felix Alcan, 1932.

To illustrate: a Scholarship Advisor for a sorority working on the campus of a major university found that, almost without exception, when her student's grades went down they had had some emotional upheaval. One had a love affair that didn't turn out right. One "A" student who's grades dropped to a "D" was found to have had an unfortunate experience which caused the sorority to ostracize her. Another's parents separated under somewhat scandalous circumstances. But the grades of these girls returned to normal once their emotional problems were straightened out.

Almost from the moment a child comes into the world, he demonstrates that he is an emotional being. Love, anger, and fear are all a part of his basic equipment. As the child

Fig. 15   *All Students are Emotional Beings*

grows and develops, his emotional stability will depend, in large measure, on how he is cared for and treated. Most of his behavior patterns will be learned. They will be acquired from the environment created by the home, the community, the school, and the church. Thorpe tells us how to achieve the desired stability in the following statement:

"ADEQUATE MATERIAL FACILITIES: The child who enjoys sufficient nourishing food, who sleeps according to his needs, and whose health is intelligently safeguarded, is likely to be characterized by emotional stability.

SECURE HOME LIFE: The child whose need for affection and personal status is adequately, but not excessively, satisfied in the home, will tend to develop a stable outlook on life. Having been provided with a feeling of "belonging", such a child is free from anxiety concerning his place in the scheme of things.

OPPORTUNITY FOR SOCIAL LIVING: Young children should be provided with the opportunity of playing and socializing happily with associates of their own age. It is through social intercourse that children learn to express their feelings and emotions in approved ways. Such experience teaches them to inhibit, as well as express, tensions in a manner acceptable to those with whom they mingle socially. Such personal status and self-realization is contingent upon social acceptance. Group activity is an essential foundation for emotional stability."[6]

It is obvious from what has been stated, that the home, community and other environmental influences do much to shape the life of the individual we meet in class. However, whether or not the teacher realizes it, the emotional stability of his students can be influenced by him to a great extent. Students will often compete with one another for teacher acceptance and approval. A smile of understanding or approval on the part of an understanding teacher, or a few words of commendation, may provide the individual with a feeling of adequacy, which he greatly needs. On the other hand, unfavorable criticism, ridicule, or general indifference may lead to a sense of inferiority or a feeling of inadequacy which could persist for many years or even a lifetime. Awareness and proper development of emotional stability and control by the student, lies directly within the range of the teacher's duties.

---

[6]Louis P. Thorpe, *Child Psychology and Development,* The Ronald Press Co., 1955.

THE SOCIAL SIDE

Essentially people are social. All of us are born dependent upon our society for existence. Physical growth, intellectual

Fig. 16

People are Essentially Social

abilities, and achievement of emotional stability, all contribute to our social development. This development is molded by the kind of social life experienced by each of us in his family, community, and cultural groups.

Just as in our physical and intellectual facets, we develop socially at different rates. However, there are at least three basic needs we all have in common: (1) All humans need to feel a sense of personal security and worth; (2) all people desire to satisfy the physiological needs such as hunger, breathe, sleep, etc.; and (3) all individuals wish to gain recognition and acceptance by others. Chapter III, Part 2 is devoted to a discussion of the necessity for understanding these basic social needs; and some of the ways of breaking down the social barriers which so often make learning impossible.

THE SPIRITUAL SIDE

In their consideration of the "whole person," many psychologists and educators would omit spiritual aspects. But to the Latter-day Saint, the spiritual side is the most funda-

Fig. 17
Spiritual Side is the Most Fundamental Part of the Individual

mental part of the individual. We feel this because we believe that all persons on earth are the literal sons and daughters of the Eternal Father; that their spirits were created by Him and existed before this life. Our mortal bodies are but the housing units for these spirits as they dwell on earth. We believe that all of us have come to earth for a purpose: to work out our salvation. This is done by learning to live correct principles through the many experiences gained here on earth. Such a revelation as "Man is saved no faster than he gains knowledge,"[7] has shown us that since the gaining of knowledge and experiences go hand in hand, our spiritual side must be considered in all that we do. Realizing this basic principle helps the Church teacher to understand that he has a definite responsibility to meet the spiritual needs of his students.

One major reason teachers have difficulty in providing for these spiritual needs is that the needs are not the same in any two persons. Therefore, we must strive to create the kind of class that will give each student the opportunity to learn and grow spiritually at his own rate. This can be accomplished when we know his needs and employ the right teaching methods to meet them.

HEREDITY AND ENVIRONMENT

Much has been written in the field of education on how heredity and environment affect the behavior of people. It is not our intent to discuss at length the role each plays in the learning process; but to point out that the attitude and behavior of the individual is affected by both.

Every person inherits certain biological characteristics from his parents. These characteristics are transmitted from parents to children by way of tiny germ cells which meet when an ovum (female) and a sperm (male) unite to form the single cell with which the individual's life begins. Thorpe explains the process when he says:

"Potentials for growth within cells initiate whatever processes are responsible for the passing on of physical traits from one generation to another. . . . The mechanisms of inheritance are controlled by Chromosomes, which have come to be called the 'bearers of heredity.' They determine the physical characteristics which the future individual will possess. . . . The chromosomes themselves, however, are composed of literally hundreds of minute particles called genes, different combinations of which are responsible for the inheritance of the various physical traits. . . . The mechanism described holds for the development of such physical characteristics as eyes, ears, feet, skin and so on."[8] (Also hair, general body size, etc.)

This suggests to the teacher that there are certain physical bounds that cannot be altered. The exception would be any unusual or abnormal environmental conditions. For example, it would be possible to separate identical twins

[7]*Teachings of the Prophet Joseph Smith*, page 217.
[8]Thorpe, Louis P., *Ibid.*

at birth, rearing one in an ideal environment as to nourishment, sun, air and the like, and he would reach the potential growth indicated by his chromosomes. If the other twin were reared in the slums, with little food, poor air, lack of sunlight and so forth, his growth could be stunted by several inches.

Another exception would be a boy or a girl who was too fat because of poor eating habits. An understanding teacher (especially a woman dealing with a girl) might encourage and guide that child to eat more wisely and improve her figure. This would eliminate some of the child's emotional problems.

But for the most part nothing can be done to change physical facts. Most of what a person is or will become is directly attributable to his environment; and the Church class is part of that environment. Study after study has shown this: one's surroundings at home, school, Church, and the community are the major factors in shaping the life of an individual. This means that the attitudes and behavior patterns of those who sit in our classes are learned, not inherited. This indicates to the teacher that a change in behavior is possible. If that change is to be a desirable one, it will be because the individual sees success and happiness for himself in what is being taught. In other words learning and motivation must go hand in hand.

HOW INDIVIDUALS LEARN

Research in the field of education and psychology reveals that people will learn what they want to learn. Further, they will have great difficulty learning that which does not interest them. Motivation is the key to successful teaching. We must create an interest first. This interest is created when the teacher, fired by his own enthusiasm, excites the class by relating the subject matter to the individual's needs. This sets the stage for motivation which is the basic component in learning.

In order to motivate, we need to pose problems that are within the range of our student's experience and abilities. These problems must be realistic, pertinent, and of immediate value to all alike. For instance, it might be how to live our

Fig. 18
Motivation is Essential to Successful Teaching

LDS standards at school, on the job, or at social functions. Standards like our Word of Wisdom, modesty in apparel, clean language and others. Try to anticipate some of the problems they will face and give them ammunition that will help them to answer the mocking questions so that they can stand firm.

Fundamental to the individual's process of learning is the depth to which he is personally involved. Educators know that learning is a process, not just an event. While there are many theories of learning, there is considerable agreement that a person must be involved in the following Five Steps of Learning, as developed by Ernest Legion,[9] before any knowledge is retained:

    1. EXPOSURE. (Unfortunately this is the full extent of too much of our present teaching. The student is a passive "hearer of the word." He has been informed and warned, but not involved.)

---

[9]Legion, Ernest M., *A Greater Generation,* The MacMillan Co., New York: 1960.

2. REPETITION. (Even the retention of factual information requires repeated exposure to the facts.)
3. UNDERSTANDING. (It is possible for a student to memorize a passage of scripture completely with little or no comprehension of either its meaning or its application in life. Understanding is an on-going and intricate experience. It is tied to maturity, insights, and creative thinking. This is the first step in the educational process where learning begins to become significant.)
4. CONVICTION. (The individual is actively and personally involved. Conviction implies the individual acceptance or rejection of a concept. Understanding leads to insights and insights to conviction. Convictions involve all the processes of personal commitment.)
5. APPLICATION. (The individual is actively and personally involved. This is the "belief and conviction that impels to action" realized. Religious and spiritual teachings and principles have no real significance until they are actively incorporated into the student's life.)

All our classes should be so taught so that the students can spread learning to cover situations and activities beyond the classroom. If they are to successfully transfer what we teaching the classroom to life situations, we should endeavor to develop proper ideas and attitudes through these five steps of learning.

POINTS TO REMEMBER:

1. Once we understand an individual's feelings, purposes, and ways of life, it is possible to become friends.
2. Every student is unique as an individual. There are infinite varieties of human beings.
3. Individuals' differences affect their ability to learn.
4. Questionaires and brief biographies are good means of getting background on students, but such information must be kept confidential.

5. Quizzes are a means of determining the knowledge level of class members and are aids in preparing lessons that will stress weak areas.

6. Be sensitive to names; be sure to handle them respectfully.

7. Non-member boys and girls are a special problem, but offer great opportunities to teachers who care about people.

8. The conscientious teacher strives to understand the individual student, the "whole" student.

9. Each individual is really five: He is physical, intellectual, emotional, social, and spiritual. But he grows and behaves as a total organism.

10. Growth, development, and behavior changes are continuous and uneven.

11. Behavior, even in a single act, is complex and grows out of many complex causes.

12. While heredity controls most of the physical side of a person, it is his environment which most influences what he is and what he will become.

13. For learning to take place, the person must become personally involved, not be a passive hearer.

14. Before knowledge is retained, the person must achieve these five steps: Exposure, repetition, understanding, conviction and application.

15. The teacher must strive to see that learning goes beyond the classroom into the lives of the students.

CHAPTER III

Creating Your Own Teaching Climate

PART I

Setting the Classroom Stage

A school teacher once asked his students why so many of them didn't go to their Church Sunday School classes. They answered, "For one thing, the teachers don't know any more about teaching than we do. And most of them don't make us feel that religion is important or interesting." George Betts gives us a key to this reaction when he says:

> "All teaching has two objectives, the subject taught and the person taught. When we teach John grammar (or religion) we teach grammar (or religion) of course; but we also teach John. And the greater of these two objectives is John. It is easy enough to attain the lesser of the objectives. Anyone of fair intelligence can master a given amount of subject matter and present it to a class; but it is a far more difficult thing to understand the individual, to master the inner secrets of the mind, the heart, and the springs of action of the learner."[1]

In Chapter II the need to gain a basic understanding of human nature was stressed. In this chapter we want to consider the importance of classroom environment, and the need for making students feel at home in the learning situation. Before we can actually teach John, as Betts suggests, we must first create an atmosphere or climate in the classroom which will stimulate a desire in John to learn. The author's father-in-law, C. F. Cheverton, was an outstanding teacher of religion

---

[1]Betts, George Herbert, *How to Teach Religion.*

Fig. 19

Create Your own Teaching Climate

for over forty years. He often gave this counsel to young, inexperienced teachers: "Religion," he said, "is caught, not taught." In other words, we as teachers, can create the situation in the classroom in which learning will take place.

How a room looks and feels is an important factor in determining the attitude of an individual when he comes to class. His feeling in the room, his attitude toward other members of the group, are all-important in deciding the kind of mind-set he develops toward learning. The proper classroom climate will enhance the learning process. In any teaching situation, there are four basic educational principles to keep in mind in achieving that climate.

FIRST, create a class in which the basic physiological needs of each class member will be met. This involves a knowledge and recognition by the teacher of the physical requirements of students. (See Part 2, Chap. II). Prior to class time, proper attention should be given to the heating, lighting, ventilation, and cleanliness of the room. Rooms can be made attractive by a little effort and concern on the part of the teacher. It is true that many buildings in which we meet are old and over-crowded. Still, much can be accomplished by alert teachers to make even these classrooms comfortable and inviting. Whether or not we are aware of it, students of all ages compare the Church classes they are experiencing with the best they have experienced in other places. This comparison may be favorable or unfavorable, and often the student is unaware he is making it.

The climate of the classroom might be compared to that in a fine restaurant. Much of the success of an outstanding meal comes from the "atmosphere" in which it is served. Fine linen, gleaming silverware, flowers on the table, the general appearance of the room, our treatment by the waiters, all these, (added to good food) make a rich and satisfying experience. The same food, bought from the same supply house and served on a "Blue-plate Special" in a "greasy-spoon cafe," would not leave us with the same feeling at all. Even the considerable saving in terms of money would not give us the same glow as the first meal. The difference is in the "climate" created by the owner of the first restaurant.

Another important physical and psychological need to consider is the seating of class members. Where possible, the arrangement of chairs, tables, desks, benches, et cetera, should be in such a way as to provide a maximum of face-to-face contact. People enjoy seeing each other's faces, not staring at the back of someone's neck. While there are times when seating people in traditional rows is helpful to a particular teaching situation, those times are few and we should not get in the habit of placing seats in this manner all the time. (See figure 20).

By arranging the seating in a semi-circle, or some other way as shown in figures 21, 22 and 23, the teacher has set the stage for class members to become better acquainted with one another. Also, he has created a classroom where the need for individual recognition can be met. Students tend to respond more naturally in classrooms where they have been made to feel at home, and where they feel they know each other. We

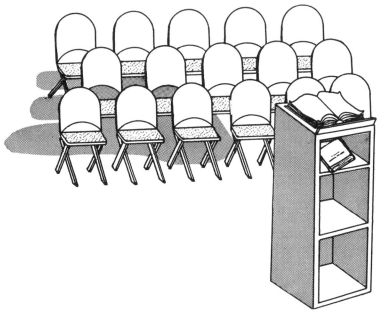

Fig. 20   *Not Always This*

Fig. 21   *But This*

Fig. 22

Or This . .

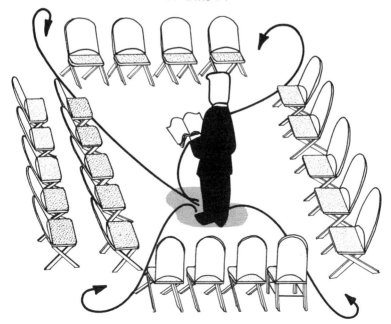

Fig. 23

Or This

all feel at ease in the presence of those we know best. Yet, if we are taken out of a social situation where we feel comfortable and placed among a group of strangers, our whole behavior pattern changes. We become more reserved and less talkative immediately. We would not begin to say or do those things that would be natural for us in a more relaxed environment. So it is with all students. Still, it is not uncommon to find individuals in many of our programs who have attended the same class for a year or more and still do not know, personally, several of their classmates. A very real part of our learning experience comes from associating with others and feeling their spirit, enthusiasm, and vitality. This is especially true in religious learning. Further, it has been my experience that in classes where a greater sense of belonging has been achieved by arranging the seating to meet student needs, the necessity for disciplinary measures has declined remarkably.

One more important thing a teacher needs to remember is to keep a permissive atmosphere in the class in order that members will feel free to express themselves. By a "permissive atmosphere" we mean an atmosphere in which the student feels he will be "permitted" at any time to voice his opinions or ideas—voice them without any fear of condescension or ridicule on the part of the teacher. This permissive atmosphere is shown most obviously by the manner in which the teacher responds when a student makes a comment or gives an opinion. Never fail to respond in some manner. Not to respond at all leaves the student dangling, and with the feeling he must have sounded like a dunce. If it happens to be his first attempt at participation, you may be sure he will hesitate before making another.

The author watched an elderly lady work for weeks to get up her courage to speak in class. One day she timidly held up her hand. The teacher permitted her to speak, but when she was finished he went on as though she had never spoken at all, ignoring entirely the comment she had made. She visibly shrank back into her shell of timidity and it is very possible that never again will she make an attempt to come out of that shell in a Church class.

A teacher does not necessarily have to agree with a student's comment. If such a comment is made, the response could be, "That's very interesting, but what about ...."? Or, "That's a good point, does the class have any other thoughts to add?" Perhaps the comment is off the subject, in which case, the student might be brought back with something like, "That's an interesting thought, but do you think it ties in with this one we're discussing?" The important thing to remember is to make as encouraging a response as possible, still keeping command of the situation and bringing out the points necessary to achieve the original goal. Let him feel that his opinions are worthy of your courteous attention and consideration, even though they might not be the most pertinent or helpful in the world.

If a teacher has made adequate preparation, is prayerful, knows the needs, interests and talents of his students, then sets the stage for learning by arranging the seating so that the best possible personal contact can be realized, he is well on his way to accomplishing his goal of effective teaching.

SECOND, keep classes "gospel-centered." By this it is not meant that the welfare or needs of the student are to be slighted, but rather that the gospel (the subject) to be taught should be the point of emphasis. All too often teachers in the Church feel that it is their responsibility or duty to become authorities on every subject—that they must be in a position to answer every possible question asked by any individual, regardless of its pertinence. This, of course, is foolish. It is extremely important that teachers be properly prepared and current in their research, but no one can be expected to know all the answers. Gospel scholarship is a desired goal for every member of the Church. It is basic Mormon philosophy! But while we are seeking new knowledge and insight, our students come to realize that even their instructors are still learning. In this framework, students are not as apt to lose their respect and admiration for the teacher who occasionally says, "I don't know," in answer to a question.

On the other hand, many persons called to teach in the Church hesitate to accept because they feel inadequate in sub-

ject matter. They may be new in the Church, or maybe just
haven't studied the gospel to the extent they feel adequate
to teach it to others. To them we offer the words of China's
most famous teacher, Confucius. He said: "He who knows some
thing and is always learning more is capable of teaching
others."[2]

A good part of the problem experienced by teachers in
both groups mentioned above, is the role that traditional education has assigned to the classroom instructor. Our immediate
understanding and definition of a traditional teacher is
a person well versed in his field—a walking dictionary and
information accumulated over many years. He is supposed to
have little or no problem in classroom technique or control.
This is one kind of teacher, but certainly not the only type.
Another that can be equally effective and successful in the
"gospel-centered" teacher. The difference between the two is in

Fig. 24
"Not always this -- the 'teacher-centered approach' ".

[2]Lowell L. Bennion, *Six Fundamentals of Good Teaching and Leadership,*
M.I.A. Association, 1961-62.

the way each plays his role. Usually the traditional teacher sits or stands at the front of the room, and through lecturing or limited class discussion imparts the information he has prepared. If a question or problem is raised that he cannot answer, his effectiveness and reputation as a teacher are somewhat challenged. Several "I don't knows" in this kind of situation can lead only to discouragement, lack of interest, and even general apathy on the part of the class. (See figure 24).

The teacher in the gospel-centered class is equally responsible for the learning that is desired. But in this approach, in a sense, he shifts the burden of "being on the spot," from himself to the entire class. They find it is equally their responsibility to seek and to find the answers to questions that arise. The teacher in the gospel-centered class becomes, in reality, the Senior student, or what Wahlquist would describe as a director of activity. In a similar situation (as described in our example of the traditional teacher) the gospel-centered person would say in all honesty "I don't know, but I will find out," or "we will seek out the solution together." And he would

Fig. 25

"Emphasis should be on the 'gospel-centered approach'."

feel neither embarrassed nor inadequate. In this method, not only do the students have a greater respect for the teacher, but they are motivated more in the learning process. Figure 25 shows how a gospel-centered class would look, in contrast to figure 24.

Further, the gospel-centered class places a greater emphasis on the "doing" phases, or the activity approach. This leads us to our THIRD principle.

THIRD, recognize the principle of the psychology of participation. We have discussed the value of seating people in such a way as to encourage more participation by providing the opportunity of meeting classmates. In turn, this causes them to feel at home and at ease. Also, it is a well-established fact that people are prone to support activities and programs in which they feel they have a part.

Once an individual has made a contribution in class, either verbally or otherwise, he has invested a part of himself. In addition to the feeling of the pride of accomplishment and recognition he experienced, the very act of contributing has opened the door for real learning to take place. A student who has participated in any kind of class activity finds it impossible to go away from that experience with anything but a positive attitude. (Provided it has been an acceptable and accepted participation, of course.) It is not in our natures to be critical of any activity for which we have in any way been responsible. This is especially obvious in the financial support of a project. Think back to the last time you helped to build a ward chapel or stake house. It was no longer "the" chapel, it was "our" chapel. And the more time and money you contributed, the greater grew your pride of "ownership."

By following the second principle of developing a gospel-centered class, students can find many opportunities to perform or to take some active part in the classroom activities, through the guidance and direction of the teacher. Instead of relying on the teacher to do all the work, they will learn to solve real problems by actually participating in discussions, projects, service projects, individual research, and so forth.

John Dewey, who was a giant in American education, made many contributions in the area of experimentalism. "Students," he said, "learn by doing."

If learning is to be meaningful, students need to see the relationship between what is being taught and the everyday problems they are experiencing. Often this can be accomplished by using group dynamics, or group activities, in solving student related problems in here-and-now situations. "Here-and-now situation" is a phrase used to describe the presentation of a concept or principle that the teacher is attempting to convey at any given time. It is presented by putting it into a life situation that is common to the experience of the student. To illustrate, if you were trying to teach the abstract concept of integrity, you might well relate it to a problem faced by every high school and college level student, that of cheating in school. For a more detailed treatment of this approach see Chapter VIII.

FOURTH, build group morale. Every teacher knows the value of team spirit. We see it at work in our local schools and

Fig. 26   *Build Group Morale*

colleges, particularly during a major sports event. The armed forces call it "Esprit de Corp." It is that certain intangible, proud feeling that makes an individual feel "he belongs." *He* belongs, he feels, to the greatest team, the most outstanding organization, the finest program in the whole country! He feels that way even when, in reality, others may be superior. It is the reason we have Texans, and Californians, and Utahns; yet when we are abroad we are Americans. It is the reason why a marine, in a fight with a sailor, will join the sailor to fight a soldier; and why all three will band together when faced with a civilian. The important thing is, to him, his IS the best.

As teachers we should try to develop this same spirit of enthusiasm, dedication and loyalty in our classes—real pride, a concern for each other, the "we" concept. When a student comes to feel that "this is our class," not Brother Blank's class, we can be reasonably sure that a basic loyalty to the group has been achieved. This is the kind of class that will provide opportunities for shared spiritual experiences; experiences

Fig. 27   *Use Audience Participation*

which will bring each member back to class week after week, not because he is commanded or forced to go, but because he would not want to miss the experience for anything. It is in this environment that real motivation is evident and where learning automatically follows. The application of the many principles of education considered in this and the remaining chapters will assist you in building strong group morale.

Good Latter-day Saints are developed out of religious experiences. Ours is not a "spectator" Church, but one of "audience participation," since it is a lay Church. We as teachers, assist in developing Church and civic leaders, training strong parents, and building good citizens. Therefore, it is necessary for us to provide opportunities for such training through the kinds of classes we conduct and the kind of climate for learning that we create in those classes.

PART 2

Breaking the Social Barrier

Previously we have discussed at some length (both in Part I of this Chapter and Part 2 of Chapter II) the organic and psychological needs of various individuals. There is another equally important and basic need in human beings that is closely related. It is the need to have fellowship. By his very nature man is social. We all know that each person is different; some are extroverts, others reserved and with-

Fig. 28

Each Person is Different

drawn. Yet, these very differences that make up the personalities in a class will have much influence on the success or failure we experience as teachers. As has been pointed out, students need to experience a sense of belonging before their minds and bodies will join forces to seek learning.

Whether he is assigned to teach an elementary, a secondary, or an adult group, it is both a responsibility and a challenge for every teacher to find ways and means of easing the social tension that is present in every class. A typical class might well have recent converts, regular attenders, inactive members back for the first time, cliques, and non-members, all visiting together in one compact classroom. A teacher who is unaware of such class make-up can do little to stimulate interest and excitement in a lesson. Before he can attempt to involve such a group in a rich religious experience, class members need to feel at ease and at home with each other.

Let's consider some possible ways of breaking the social barrier so that individuals and groups can be motivated to learn more effectively. One method that has always proved helpful is making sure that every class member has had an opportunity to be introduced to every other member. It is assumed that the teacher would create the setting for this activity. By standing at the door as class members arrive, the teacher is in an excellent position to shake hands with every

Fig. 29   *Breaking the Social Barrier*

person and ask his name. If the class members are not well acquainted, the group could form a reception line to his right as each member is greeted at the door by the teacher or a class officer. As Student "A" arrives, he is greeted by the host, then steps to the host's side thus beginning the line. Student "B" arrives, speaks to the host, student "A", then takes his place in line. By the time all class members have entered the room, each has gone through the line and has been in the line, thus has met every other class member. It is amazing how just getting to know those around you will increase the desire to participate and discuss.

Another technique which has proved successful might be called the "unique accomplishment" approach. This is how it works: A blank piece of paper is handed to each student who then writes two or three of his "unique" accomplishments, things he feels he has done or achieved that probably no one else in the class has done. For instance, the author might write "I walked across the Island of Guam barefooted," or "I pitched to Lou Gehrig when I was thirteen." The entire exercise need not take more than three to five minutes.

Outside of class the teacher takes the responses and compiles them on a single dittoed or mimeographed sheet, omitting the names of the students. In the period following the collection of the material (and using only five or six minutes) the teacher can involve his students in an interesting, verbal guessing game as to which accomplishments belong to which students. It is a fascinating way to learn a lot about people in a short time, and the conversational carry-over after class is wonderful. This information is invaluable to the teacher in adding to the interest-inventory of each student.

Listed below are some other suggestions which will aid you in the week-to-week task of keeping the social barrier down and creating the right kind of climate. Obviously, the success of carrying out these suggestions rests with the individual teacher. Knowledge not used is of little value. His attitude, enthusiasm, and preparation will determine how successful he, and his class, will be.

Fig. 30   *Extend Friendships Beyond the Class*

Fig. 31   *Show Him that You are Interested*

Suggested Ways of Breaking the Social Barrier
with Students of All Ages

1. At class meeting have an active member of the class sit with the person you are trying to integrate. The active member, at your request, can share the responsibility of helping to involve the newcomer. This is the "Big Brother" idea in action.

2. Extend your own friendships beyond the limits of the class meeting, and the boundaries of the ward building.

3. When going to Church, or any other meeting in which you and your class members will be together, ask one or more of your students to ride with you. Or ask if you may ride with them.

4. When you see a class member alone, stop and talk to him. (Be sure you call him by name). Show him that you are interested in him. No one minds being asked questions about himself.

5. Call your class members on the telephone on any pretext what-so-ever and talk to them for a minute or two.

6. Send cards to students on special occasions: Birthdays, Christmas, etc.

7. Invite several class members to your home for an informal afternoon or evening. Invite all of them if it is a small class, otherwise a few at a time until all have been invited. This can involve any kind of activity which is appropriate and possible.

8. Learn to give a little love—and don't be afraid or ashamed to accept some from them. Above all, try to be interested and friendly.

9. Place a picture of one of your students on the bulletin board each week, with a short description of personality, interests and aspirations.

10. Have class members pair off and allow partners ten or fifteen minutes to give a brief sketch or history

of his partner to the class. Have both stand before the group while one describes the other.

11. Have members of the class count off: 1, 2, 3, 4, etc., to form groups of four or five people. In each group each student takes his turn twice at being 'on the spot.' He stands before the group and, the first time around, each member asks him a personal question. The second time around they ask him a question in a given field, such as religion, sports, etc. In questioning and answering each person calls the other by both names.

12. A very effective method, especially to culminate a special occasion or a particularly fine experience, is a class testimony meeting. Remember always, fellowship is brotherhood in the gospel.

There are many techniques which can be utilized by the teacher to reach his students and make them feel at ease. We have listed but a few of them. The method or approach is not the important thing, but rather the direct involvement and activity of every class member. There are always those in every class who are willing and eager to participate in everything. But effective teachers aim to have the involvement of all. As Galileo said: "You cannot teach a man anything; you can only help him find it within himself." This then becomes our immediate concern: To create a classroom atmosphere that sets the stage for real learning and discovery, and to remove the social barrier that keeps students from participating.

POINTS TO REMEMBER:

1. There are four major points in setting the classroom stage for learning:

    A. Meet the physiological needs of cleanliness and comfort.

    B. Keep the class gospel-centered, instead of teacher centered.

    C. Recognize and utilize the psychology of participation: When the student invests a part of himself by participating, he will be both more interested and less critical.

    D. Build group morale by cultivating the "we" concept.

2. Students must feel at ease before learning can take place. Therefore, we must break down the social barriers that keep students apart.

3. Ways to break down the social barrier:

    A. Introduce each student to every other member.

    B. Pair off students and let them do brief histories of each other.

    C. Occassionally, let the period culminate in a testimony meeting.

    D. Love them and help them to love one another.

4. Methods are less important than getting students involved.

CHAPTER IV

Where Am I Going?

What is a purpose? Is there a difference between a purpose and an objective? If so, do we need both? A most succinct answer to these questions was given by a very young teacher who said, "My objective is where I am going, and my purpose is why I am going there."

Fig. 32 *My Objective is Where I am Going. My Purpose is Why I am Going There.*

Though purpose and objective are often used synonymously, they are not exact synonyms. The gospel teacher will find it useful to keep the difference (as defined above) clearly in mind, because he has need of both. It is of supreme importance that he have an objective or goal. It is equally important that he know WHY he is trying to reach that goal or end.

"Why" we do anything is more important than "what" we do. Ask a basketball player what his objective is and he will probably tell you it is to make as many baskets as possible. If you ask him why, his answer would be to win the game. What would there be to the game if there were no points to be made, no winning or losing? This then, the "why," makes the game of basketball meaningful, or the game of football, or life itself. The reason for trying is the purpose that gives meaning to life. As Royal Garff, an authority on Speech, has said, "The secret of success is purpose."

It is part of the obligation of any gospel teacher to be sure his students know that the objective of the Latter-day Saint is to have joy and happiness; that the Plan of Salvation is the means by which he can reach that objective; and that his purpose in seeking that goal is that he may have eternal life.

THERE ARE THREE KINDS OF OBJECTIVES

There will always be more than one objective in any teaching situation. Let us consider three major types:

1. The big over-all objective. In the gospel the teacher is to help his students gain testimonies and eternal life.
2. The objective or objectives of the year's work or course of study. These objectives are usually provided by the course writers. Objectives such as Jesus is the Christ, or Joseph Smith is a Prophet, etc.
3. The objective of each specific lesson. Again, these objectives are most often supplied by the writer of the lesson materials. But there are times when the teacher will need to develop his own or add to the suggested ones: For example, to develop faith in Christ and His teachings.

For instance, in the MIA Speech Department it is stated like this: The over-all objective of the MIA is to help young people build testimonies for themselves; the basic objective of the Speech Department is to make these testimonies articulate. Then the specific objective of a weekly lesson might be to teach the students how to bear a testimony, or deliver a speech, or read a scripture.

In working on any specific objective we should always keep in mind the objective of the year and the over-all goal.

Fig. 33   *All Sources Lead to the Prime Objective*

However, enrichment materials, visual aids, et cetera, should be chosen with the idea that they pertain to the objective of a specific lesson. For example, if you were teaching a course in Church History, one objective of the year might be to "Bring to the students an understanding of the sacrifices of our pioneer ancestors, and the high ideals that motivated them".

Then on a specific lesson dealing with the exodus from Nauvoo, the enrichment material might be faith-promoting stories of the forbears of members from the class. Especially to be emphasized would be those stories in which the people explained their motives for following Brigham Young.

ONE MAJOR IDEA FOR ONE LESSON

While each lesson may have more than one idea to consider, only one **major** idea should be finally developed. The other ideas should all lead to the understanding of that one major thought or concept. But trying to get too many ideas in one lesson remains one of the greatest pitfalls for the lay teacher. He often tries to teach all there is to know at one time. For instance, such subjects as faith, God, the Priesthood,

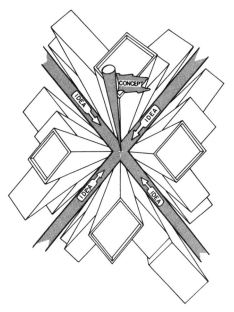

Fig. 34

All Ideas should Lead to the Understanding of one Major Concept

gospel ordinances, et cetera are much too broad to be covered in one session. It is necessary to choose one facet or phase of such big topics to cover in a single lesson. If you could teach only one thing about God, what would you choose to teach? That God is the creator of all things? That He is anthropomorphic, that is, that He has a body, parts, and passions? That He reveals Himself to man through His prophets? That He is our actual spiritual father? That He loves us as individuals? You can see how difficult it would be to cover thoroughly any one of these in a single class period, let alone cover all of them.

One further point: Be sure that the objective which you choose is on the level of your class. That is, the objective for a class of eighteen year old students could hardly be to memorize a passage of scripture. Yet for a class in Primary that might be a very good one. Or, you could not expect a Primary student to understand the term "anthropomorphic", but to high school or college students the use of the term in the objective might give them an understanding previously lacking, as well as piquing their imaginations.

HOW TO DETERMINE YOUR OBJECTIVE

Many of our lesson materials include stated objectives for both the year and for each lesson. This is done for the guidance of the teacher, to help him stay on the desired track. Even if the objective is clearly stated, the teacher needs to be sure he understands exactly what he is expected to accomplish. Also, he may wish to include an extra objective of his own for a special purpose. That is, he may wish to emphasize one part of the objective, or of the course, because of a particular weak-

Fig. 35 *A Single Lesson is Only a Part of the Course Objective*

ness in the knowledge of his group. However, care must be taken to reach the objective laid out by the Church. As Woodruff says: "It is more important to follow the Church's stated objective than it is to use any particular material for it".[1]

In cases where no objectives are stated in the lesson materials, the teacher must decide what these objectives are to be, keeping in mind the over-all goal and the goal of his particular organization. (For instance, the main goal of the

---

[1]Asahel Woodruff, Ibid: p. 117.

Primary is to prepare our children for baptism and the Priesthood). Then read the materials through for the entire year to
get an over-all picture of the year's work. Only then try to
decide what you think is the main idea for the year. Jot down
several ideas as they come to mind. From them formulate one
major idea which you feel is most needed by your group.

Sometimes no objective is stated for the year, but objectives are given for the individual lessons. This makes it easier
to determine what major objective the Church had in mind.
For example, one of the courses for the Visiting Teacher's
Message in Relief Society is titled "Truths to Live by From
the Doctrine and Covenants". No goal for the year's work is
stated as such. However, considering the title, and reading
through the objectives given for each lesson, an objective
might be formulated thus: "To show that the living truths
found in the Doctrine and Covenants are useful guides in
today's living".

UNIT AND LESSON PLANNING GUIDES

Once you have determined the objective for the year, read
again the general outline for the year's work, the Table of
Contents. Read it to decide if this work can be broken logically
into three to five portions. That is, are the individual lessons
grouped into "units" of four or five chapters? Some authors
do this obviously, others merely infer it. If yours are inferred
only, then you should try to group them yourself. The reason
for this unit grouping is to find the several main concepts
covered in the year and plan your smaller lessons as a unit.
It's like climbing a long flight of stairs and coming to a landing
every so often — it gives one a chance to look back at what
has been accomplished, to see if one has reached the objective.
Also, it gives one a chance to look at the next "flight" and plan
how to reach the next landing. (See Figure No. 36.)

An excellent example of this unit breakdown is Bennion's
Gospel Doctrine Manual for 1961 called *Teachings of the New
Testament*. He has put the forty-four lessons into eight units.
These range from three chapters in his "Introduction", through
as many as ten in his "social Ideals in the New Testament",
down to only one in the last unit. As you see, it is not a

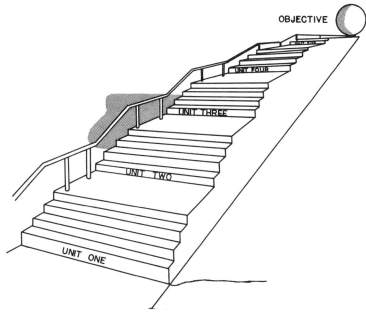

Fig. 36   *Unit Planning*

matter of dividing the number of lessons into so many equal groups. It is a matter of dividing the material into logical sections so that it might be studied more easily. This may take a little time and study if the author of the manual has not done it for you, but you will find it time well spent.

Lesson planning is quite another problem. In Speech we say, "a speech is like a journey, it must have a destination". This is equally true of a lesson, for each must be traveling toward a specific end. Each must have a plan, for as Garff says, your plan is your map that guides you to your destination. There are many lesson plans, and many very good ones. Both Bennion and Woodruff show excellent examples in their teaching manuals. Or you may want to develop your own. Most good ones have much in common.

The one preferred by the writers is essentially Bennion's "Five Steps", which is used in his manual for the Teacher Director of the MIA: *Six Essentials of Good Teaching and Leadership.* Also, one may vary the plan for different lessons as the material lends itself to different development. For in-

Fig. 37   *Your Lesson Plan is the Map that Guides You*

stance, a lesson in which you plan a lot of discussion by class members, will of necessity have to be planned with many questions in the outline. This is because discussions need leading questions to get them started and to keep them going. The important thing is to have a plan and to use it:

FIND A PLAN THAT WORKS AND THEN
WORK THAT PLAN

LET'S LOOK AT A SAMPLE

The following sample lesson will show you how to get a lesson planned on paper. This is one of the great frustrations of the lay teacher, to plan a beautiful lesson on paper and have it flop in the classroom because the students did not respond in the way the teacher expected.

Here is one plan for a lesson on the Word of Wisdom for seventeen and eighteen year olds. It is called the question-answer-discussion technique. On the left will be the Five Steps of Preparation; on the right, the material to be used to develop Step 4, Main Ideas. There are three main ideas used to develop the lesson.

SAMPLE LESSON ON THE WORD OF WISDOM
For 17-18 Year-olds

STEP 1: BRAINSTORMING:
(What ideas come to mind as you read? What questions?)
A. Old subject, needs fresh approach.
B. What about n e w scientific facts?
C. Why aren't milk products mentioned?
D. How much of the spirit of the W of W should we teach youth?
E. "Whole body full of light," D&C 88:67. Will W of W help?
F. Should we stick to teaching tea, coffee, tobacco and alcohol?
G. European doctor now says 3 tbsp. of wheat a day will cure cancer. Will it prevent it?
H. Why didn't Joseph Smith simply tell us to use the best information available to guide us in staying away from harmful food and drugs?

STEP 2: STATE OBJECTIVE:
To help them to understand that the W of W is a spiritual principle that contains a law, not of deprivation, but of health, knowledge, and blessings.

STEP 3: FIND A BEGINNING:
European Doctor who says wheat will cure cancer. (Fresh approach and will lead into inspiration of Prophet.)

STEP 4: MAIN IDEAS TO DEVELOP:
A. Inspiration of the Prophet Joseph.
B. The "spirit" of the W of W is not law, but it is wisdom.
C. Value of W of W today.

STEP 4: MAIN IDEAS TO DEVELOP:
Point 1: (Development:) IN-SPIRATION OF THE PROPHET JOSEPH SMITH:
Illustrations, quotes, questions, etc.:
A. Check D&C Commentary and Widtsoe's W of W for material to use.
B. Real aloud from Commentary if desirable at time.
C. When was revelation given? 2-27-1833. Under what circumstances?
D. How much was known of nutrition at that time? Vitamins? Protein as building bricks for the body?
E. Watch for any new stories on nutrition in papers and magazines; ask students for any they've seen.

Point 2: ON SPIRIT OF LAW:
A. We are told to gain all knowledge.
B. Is knowledge of any value if it is not used?
C. Should we take advantage of new scientific facts discovered? For instance: WofW does not mention milk or cheese as being valuable. Should we not use them then?
D. Neither does it mention drugs as such. Does this mean we are free to use them? Dope?
E. Read D & C 88:67, "Whole body full of light" and discuss in relation to W of W.

Point 3: VALUE OF W OF W TODAY:
A. Do we have greater or less need of health - law guidance

STEP 5: CONCLUSION:

Summary and my testimony of living the W of W in worldly affairs. W of W is a law given us by inspiration for our benefit, and has been confirmed over and over by science today. The "spirit" of the W of W is not a law, but it is wisdom to take advantage of new knowledge. This makes the W of W of immense value in today's living.

today? (Vast quantity of new products).

B. What should we do when a doctor or a superior officer orders us to drink stimulants as a "relaxant"? (Tell story of two boys in army, i.e. find an example.)

C. Is it necessary to drink in business? School? Socially? Have them give examples. Follow with Ezra Taft Benson's testimony, and a couple of personal examples.

SELECTING MATERIAL FOR CLASSROOM USE

This topic will be covered in detail in Chapters VI and IX, but two points should be kept in mind:

1. All material selected must lead toward the objective. Tangents are the primrose paths of teachers and speakers. No matter how interesting, how funny, how useful, or even how true a story or point may be, do

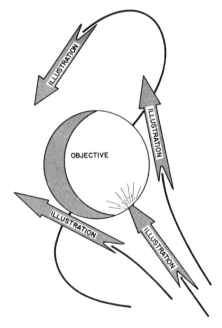

Fig. 38   *All Materials must lead toward the Objective*

not use it unless it carries the lesson toward the objective. Nowhere have we heard it stated more succinctly than by Woodruff in Chapter 13: "How do you accomplish an objective: There are two simple rules that come first in this matter:

1. You have to Begin with it, Stay with it, End with it— IT IS the lesson.

2. Everything else (material etc.) has to be used WHEN it helps the objective, WHERE it helps the objective, In the manner WHICH helps the objective, AND NOT AT ALL IF IT DOESN'T HELP!

2. Care must be exercised constantly to be sure that all materials used are suitable and in proper balance. Often it is interesting and useful to find verification of a gospel concept from a scientific source, or to find a fresh approach in a current magazine article or news story. But beware of letting such outside materials become the major part of your lesson. For example, a young teacher was to give a lesson on speech delivery and how to use one's hands, eyes, body, etc., to give animation. In approximately five minutes he disposed of the excellent material provided in his manual, then spent the rest of the period on how the eyes functioned. This he read to them from a book he was currently studying because of an eye problem. His personal problem made this material intensely interesting to him.

NOT AN OVERWHELMING PROBLEM

None of the steps involved in this chapter are difficult in themselves. As the old saying goes, "Yard by yard it's hard, but inch by inch it's a cinch". Now that you are aware of the need for both an objective and a purpose, you will find yourself mentally looking for them as you start on a lesson or a new course. Nor will the three kinds of objectives be hard to locate now that you have an idea how to look. Even units and lesson plans will not seem so incomprehensible now that you have seen their value and have some idea how to construct them.

The important thing is to have a purpose, have an objective, have a plan. Each of them will help you to teach a better lesson and teach it more effectively.

POINTS TO REMEMBER:

1. Our objective tells us where we are going; our purpose tells us why.

2. There are three types of objectives: the over-all, the yearly course, and the weekly or daily.

3. If your course materials do not state your objectives, work them out for yourself. Read all the course outlines and decide what the main ideas are for the year, and for each lesson.

4. Break down the year's work into units or groups of lessons which can be studied as a whole.

5. Make a written plan, a road map, for each lesson. Find a plan that works, then work that plan.

6. All material used must lead toward the objective.

7. "Yard by yard it's hard, inch by inch it's a cinch!"

CHAPTER V

"Abstract" Is My Pink Horse

PART I
Defining Our Terms

"My horse is pink and has five legs," said a professor friend, to explain that when one talks in unfamiliar terms he must first define those terms.

"No one can accept an idea until it is couched in words he can accept," said another, explaining his unorthodox use and grouping of words.

Having heard so many of our academically untrained Church teachers struggle through explanations of "principles" and "abstract concepts," it occurs to us to try to explain them from a different and less academic approach.

Let us start by defining some "pink horses." Since this is a problem of semantics, let us start with that. Semantics is a study of the meaning of words. Semantically speaking, what a word means to you is the sum total of the experience you have had with that word. For instance, if your total experience with a river is the rushing, tumbling torrent of the Rogue River in Oregon, you will have difficulty understanding that the dry paved bed of the Los Angeles is also a river. To the born and bred Angeleno the Rogue River would be a totally new concept; while to a Civil Engineer with both wide knowledge and experience, "river" would include the concept of vast power as well.

This is one reason why a teacher needs to use example after example to illustrate a new term. Each student must be able to find something familiar in the illustrations, something which ties in with his own experience, if he is to understand the new.

THE WORD "PRINCIPLE"

Several words are widely used to describe or explain "principle." Since "abstract" is the one most often used,

Fig. 39

Abstract

let us next define it. We are concerned only with the adjective and that in a limited sense. Webster says that abstract is something considered a part from an actual object. Here he is speaking of such things as abstract truth, or an ideal. Abstract expresses a quality which is not concrete, a quality like honesty; or whiteness in the sense of blankness.

"Intangible" is another word often used to describe principle and abstract. A tangible thing is a substantial object having substance. A tangible asset may be a building, such as a book or a table. A thing capable of being realized by the senses. Therefore, an intangible would be something *not* having substance. A tangible asset may be a building, a piece of land, or a machine. An intangible asset would be a good reputation, one's integrity, or the goodwill of a business.

Fig. 40

Tangible

For a Latter-day Saint a tangible benefit of keeping the Word of Wisdom would be better health and a clearer mind. An intangible benefit would be a strengthening of testimony, a greater resistance to the temptations of the appetites, and the blessings that come from obedience to the guidance of the Lord.

THE WORD "CONCEPT"

Now, let us look at "concept." A concept is an idea. Your conception of a thing is your idea or ideas concerning it. For example, as Latter-day Saints we conceive God to be our Father, literally the Father of our spirits. We conceive Him to have all the good attributes of our earthly fathers in a perfect degree. People of other faiths have an entirely different conception. To some He has no body, He is only spirit. To others He is merely a power diffused through the universe. Now God is not a concept, but these are our concepts or ideas about Him, based upon our total experience with Him.

Fig. 41   *Concepts*

Fig. 42   *Principle*

Having defined the terms we will be using, let us return to our basic idea of explaining a principle.

A principle is an abstract concept. It is not a tangible object like a chair. A principle is a description or an explanation, it is not an act. For instance, the act of baptism, or an explanation of *how*, by *whom*, *when*, or *where* is not a statement of the principle of baptism. The principle is concerned only with the *why*.

Because it is easier to explain the *what*, than the *why*, many teachers fail to teach principles at all.

The *what* and *when* and so forth, may be a necessary prelude to the *why*, as when teaching a child about prayer; but a teacher must never get so involved in the *what* that he fails to reach the more important *why*. For only the *why* is a statement of the principle.

Like baptism, mechanical obedience is an act. It is not a statement of the abstract concept or principle of obedience. Children can be taught to obey either because they have faith in the one teaching, or because they are afraid of the consequences. For example, it is easy to teach a child not to touch a hot stove. He can be put close enough without burning him to make him understand it would be painful to touch. But this would not teach him anything of the principle of heat. It would remain an act of mechanical obedience.

A PRINCIPLE IS A STATEMENT OF RELATIONSHIP

A principle is also a statement of relationship. For instance, the principle of obedience is a statement of the relationship of the cause and effect of obedience on our lives; a statement of *why* we obey the laws of God and man.

An example is found in chronic traffic violators. They are people with no understanding of the principle behind traffic regulations. They do not understand the relationship between the traffic laws and safety; not only their own safety, but that of others as well.

Just so, those who consistently fail to obey the laws of God, fail also to understand the relationship between obedience to the laws of God and their own well-being. Nor do they understand that same relationship to the salvation of their fellow men.

The commandment to love our fellow men falls into the same category. We react to the effects of love-actions, that is, we feel good when someone does something nice for us. But this will not make us love the rest of our fellow men unless we understand the principle of love. We find it difficult or impossible to love people that we do not know, or who are dirty, or drunkards and so forth, because we fail to understand the principle behind the commandment.

UNDERSTANDING NOT NECESSARY TO USE OF PRINCIPLE

It is obvious that we do not need to understand a principle to invoke it or use it to a limited extent. We can get water from a faucet by turning the handle, it is not necessary to understand the principle of water pressure.

A wind that we cannot see, can blow down a solid wall of concrete. We see the wall fall, and feel the pressure of the wind, without understanding the principle which makes the wall tumble.

We can see a block of ice melt in the rays of the sun without understanding the principle of heat. We cannot see the heat, but we can feel it and see its action on the ice. We do not have to understand the principle to "see" this much, nor do we have to understand the principle to put it to use. Many a man used gravity to bring his water down the hill long before the word came into being.

Just as some blessings will come from mechanical obedience, so we can get some results from employing any principle we do not understand. But until we do understand the principle, we can never reap the full harvest. We will not act, we will only react as a child or even an animal.

A child or an animal will warm himself at the edge of a fire, but draw back from any contact with it because it hurts. A man who understands the principle of heat will harness that fire and use it to his advantage for cooking, heating, or power.

Everyone knew that apples fell from trees, but only after Newton explained the principle involved was it put to full use. Mankind continues to reap the benefits. So it is with all principles. Until we learn the *why*, the relationship between life and the principle, we cannot fulfill the purposes for which we were put on the earth. For as Woodruff says, "One who aspires to celestial life must learn the deeper explanations of life which usually take the form of abstract eternal laws and forces. He must learn the WHY in addition to the WHAT."[1]

This is why the Prophet Joseph Smith told us "A man cannot be saved in ignorance": For unless he understands the principle he will not ACT (i.e. be motivated) he will only REACT as a child or an animal.

The same is true of all the principles of the gospel: faith, repentance, baptism, and love of God. Until we learn the *why*, until we understand the relationship of these principles to life, we will not be motivated to live our lives in accordance with these principles. Until we can live the principles, we will continue to fall short of our potential goal, which is eternal life. Therefore, let us learn the principles, then let us teach them.

---

[1]Woodruff, Asahel D., ibid, p. 145.

PART 2

How To Teach a Principle

If there is a simple formula for the teaching of principles, it might be stated thus:

State the principle, then climb to understanding up the steps of example. (See Figure 43.)

Fig. 43   *State the Principle — Then Climb the Steps of Example to Understanding*

It may be useful to re-examine Part 1 of this chapter with the above illustration in mind. For, as a student once remarked on hearing the explanation of a principle, "You seem to be explaining the 'principle' of a principle." This seems to be a valid observation and may add some clarity for the teacher.

HOW TO BRING UNDERSTANDING

Understanding will come to your students when they "see" the relationship between the "words" of the principle and life as it is. Therefore, the way to teach a principle is to show that relationship to them by example; example; example; plus constant repetition of the "words" of the concept.

Examples are a form of experience, and only experience with the concept in action will lead to understanding of the stated concept. These needed experiences will come to us gradually throughout our lives, but in a classroom we can clarify and lay a foundation for actual experiences through the use of the vicarious experience of examples.

In the case of a child, and a very simple concept, he can be led actually to have the experience in class. For instance, the concept of sharing, as part of the larger principle of love, is one that is constantly demonstrated in Primary and Junior Sunday School. But if the experience is not conducive to being produced in class, then the re-told experience of someone else is an excellent substitute. The best "someone else" would be a member of the class or the teacher; the second best, would be someone each person in the class would recognize, such as Brigham Young, General Eisenhower, the Bishop, and so forth. The third best choice would be an experience taken from the scriptures, such as Nephi leading his people to the American continent as an example of faith in action, or Moses leading his people to the promised land as an example of the principle of obedience. Number four in preference would be a story from any authentic book or magazine which was a clear illustration of the principle being discussed. What could be used would depend on the complexity of the concept, as well as the age and purpose of the group being taught. Such visual aids as movies and film strips are often valuable if wisely used, and their use will be discussed in a later chapter.

There is a tendency to forget that adults need these story-experiences as much as children or young people do. Thus we find some Gospel Doctrine classes being taught, not only in a dull manner, but without any transfer of learning. Probably the greatest difference in the teaching of the various age groups would be in the amount of actual experiences of the class members which could be brought into use. The basic formula is the same for all ages. The method would vary in the complexity of the principle and the experience of the group.

CLARIFY THE ACT OR WORD

Especially with the younger ages, it is often necessary to explain the *what* of the action before the *why* or principle can be explained. For example, the words joy, gratitude, humility, baptism. A child, or even a teenager, may have no knowledge of what these words mean. The preliminary step then, would be to clarify what the act is, or the word means. Then the teacher could begin on the more difficult process of explaining the *why*, that is, the relationship of the act or word to actual living.

To illustrate, in any study of the principle of baptism, the *what, where, when, how,* and *by whom* would need to be clear in the minds of the students before any fruitful discussion could take place on the principle, the *why* of baptism. However, since the what, the where, and so forth are so much easier to understand and to teach, there is the constant temptation to let discussion of these use the whole time available. Many times this is done inadvertantly because an inexperienced teacher does not clearly understand this abstract *why* himself. As has often been said, we cannot teach that which we do not have.

SELECTING THE BEST CONCEPT TO TEACH

Some writers of course materials do not state clearly the objective of a lesson. Then the teacher must decide which is the most important message of the lesson, and what concepts to teach in order to reach it; that is, to put it into the lives of the students. Much care needs to be exercised to be sure we choose worthwhile concepts, not just "interesting" ones.

For instance, the basic principles of the gospel are necessary to salvation. We cannot reach the Celestial Kingdom without understanding repentance, the Priesthood, free agency, and temple marriage. It follows that the basic principles of the gospel *must* be taught if we are to consider that we are keeping the commandment of the Lord to teach the gospel to our families and those for whom we are responsible as teachers. If one is in doubt as to which are the fundamental doctrines, the Articles of Faith and the four Standard Works of the Church are valuable checkpoints.

There are many other principles which are just as true, but not so necessary to our salvation. For example it is not really necessary for us to understand how the Urim and Thummin worked in order for us to work out our salvation. Though the principle upon which the Urim and Thummin works is as true a principle as, for instance, the principle of obedience.

Still other areas such as those called "the mysteries," are very interesting upon which to speculate. In almost any class it is easy to get a lively discussion on one of them. But they are totally unnecessary for us to understand *at this time.* When they *are* needful to our salvation, the Lord will clarify them in the usual manner. In the meantime, let us not waste the valuable and brief time of our class periods which would be so much more profitably put to use on the more basic principles which *have* been given to us and which are so necessary for us to learn.

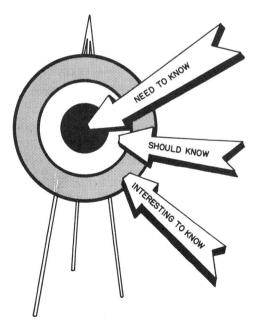

Fig. 44 *Class Time Should be Devoted to Learning Principles We Need to Know*

Another pitfall is choosing an unimportant concept from a complex one, to the exclusion of the more useful facets. To illustrate: a young member of a Teacher Training class was given an assignment to work up a lesson on the Word of Wisdom for a class of nine year old boys.

In her desire to do something new and different with this oft-repeated subject, she decided to concentrate on but two facets of the Word of Wisdom. One was that "tobacco is for sick cattle." To illustrate this she found a large magazine picture in color of Paul Bunyon's great blue ox Babe. This was pasted on a larger square of cardboard. Then, with letters of various sizes clipped from newspaper headlines, the words of the text were spelled out across the bottom of the cardboard. The bright blue "cow" did look sick indeed, and the nine year old boys to whom it was subsequently shown, were much impressed.

The second facet chosen was "—hot drinks are not for the body or the belly." Ignoring the more important factor of the stimulants involved, the new teacher took to the class two thermos bottles: One filled with boiling water, the other with ice water, together with two small bowls. Pouring the contents of the thermos bottles into the bowls, she walked down the rows of students having each one put his hand into the boiling water, then in the ice water. At the same time carefully explaining that if this heat and cold could not be borne by the hand, how much less possible would it be for the tender lining of the stomach to bear. Again the boys were intrigued and impressed.

The teacher of the training class was also impressed, and enchanted with the imagination shown on the assignment. However, the experienced teachers and leaders who saw the original demonstration maintained that the student-teacher had missed the point of the Word of Wisdom almost entirely, and would lead the children astray in their thinking. The blue cow part had some merit, but they felt that even that tended to overshadow the point of a very serious subject. That certainly was not the intent of the student-teacher and may or may not have been a valid criticism. However, the most severe criticism centered around the hot and cold portion of the demonstration.

Though stung by the criticism, the beginning teacher dismissed most of it as "old fogy" stuff. Her own thinking and development had to proceed for some time before she realized completely how unwise her choice of concept had been. The story is told here because it is an excellent example of the point being discussed: That it is very easy to choose an "interesting" facet of a concept to the exclusion of the more worthwhile and needful portions of a complex principle.

LITTLE CONCEPTS FROM BIG ONES

In teaching, as in speaking, there is always the temptation to try to cover too much territory in a single lesson. In the teaching of abstract concepts it is vitally important that this temptation be avoided. Properly presented, one concept is usually enough for a whole lesson. Trying to teach more than one obscures the principle and compounds the confusion.

Practice choosing a single specific concept from a larger, more complex one. For instance, if you could teach only *one* concept about God in a lifetime, what would it be? Would you teach Him as the Creator? As a loving Father? That He has an actual body of flesh and bones? That He loves each of us as an individual? Any one of these is a sufficiently large concept for one or several lessons. If you could choose only one, which would be that important *one* to you or your class? Try this with any of the great complex principles, keeping in mind how confusing it would be if you were teaching one and then started giving examples of one of the other concepts. It is here that the lesson objective plays such an important role.

Another useful device is to take a principle like faith and make a list of all the smaller concepts of this complicated principle, in order of their importance. (See Chapter IV, Brainstorming.) Try this with several of the basic principles of the gospel. It is excellent practice in gearing the mind to seeing and choosing specific facets to develop from a larger whole. Also, to see the relative importance of each of the smaller concepts that go to make up that whole.

The more study and thought put upon this complicated process of learning and teaching abstract concepts, the more obvious it appears that understanding comes only when one truly can "see" the relationship between the "words" and life itself. Therefore, we can teach a principle by stating the principle, then climbing to understanding up the steps of examples of that principle in action on an individual's life. Because the gospel is composed of the principles of salvation, it follows that we must learn those principles if we are to *attain* salvation. As teachers, we must see that our students learn those principles too.

POINTS TO REMEMBER:

1. If you would use unfamiliar terms, first define those terms.

2. A principle is not an act; it is the *why*.

3. A principle is an explanation of a relationship.

4. It is not necessary to understand a principle to employ it or to use it in a limited way.

5. When we understand the *why*, we can be motivated to act.

6. Only in living the principles will we find salvation. This explains why we cannot be saved in ignorance.

7. To show the relationship between the "words" of the principle and life, it is necessary to show the principle in action by the use of many examples.

8. Sometimes it is necessary to teach the *what* before we can teach the *why*, which is the principle. However, care should be exercised that the *what* does not exclude the *why*.

9. Further care must be exercised in choosing worthwhile, instead of "interesting," concepts to teach. Salvation, not speculation, is our ultimate goal.

10. To avoid confusion, choose only one concept for each lesson.

CHAPTER VI

A Plan for Power: Preparation Plus Prayer

Teaching a lesson successfully is like taking a trip—you have to know where you are going before you start, and where you have been after you have been there. With this thought in mind, let us examine two basic rules in teaching and see how they can be applied to lesson planning:

1. PREPARATION: How far ahead do you read in the course you are teaching? Do you read the entire

Fig. 45 *Preparation is the First Rule to Good Lesson Planning*

course, or are you a marathon runner who jumps each hurdle as he comes to it? Preparation includes reading far enough ahead (preferably the entire manual or book) so that you will know exactly where the course is taking you and how each lesson fits into the general plan. After all, if you know that you are going to New York, but don't know that you are going by the Southern Route, you may get on a train to Yellowstone Park because the color scheme in the club car is more pleasing to you. So read ahead far enough to know your ultimate destination and the route by which you plan to get there. There is no substitute for knowing where you are going.

2. ORGANIZATION: All teachers are extremely busy people. In addition to the heavy demands made on their time, they are expected to become proficient in many areas of the gospel. Teachers who meet these demands successfully, attribute their success to effective organization of their time and their materials. To do this, they must have materials on hand to meet the following needs:

Fig. 46 *Effective Organization is Important to Lesson Planning*

    A. Individual lesson preparations.

    B. Supplementary materials for each lesson (books and source material).

    C. Enrichment materials for both teacher and student.

It is important that we develop some kind of reference program for ourselves through which we can systematically gather and keep available enrichment materials to add life to our lessons. While no one system will work for every teacher, one main requirement for any filing system is that it should keep materials readily accessible. Unless you can find what you have, or what you need at any particular time, your material will have little value. So either make an index file or a bonfire. A card index will tell you what you have and where it can be found, and it is said that your filing system is only as good as your index. The following are some suggested systems which any of us can make and keep up. Usually you will want two systems, preferably more.

    1. A CARD FILE FOR BRIEF QUOTATIONS. Use either 3 x 5 cards or the 4 x 6 size. Write out the

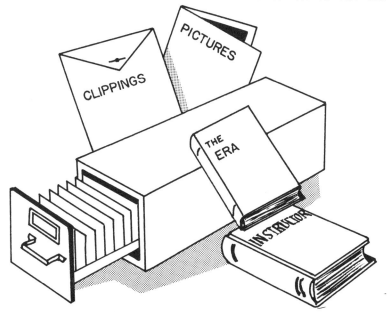

Fig. 47   *Card Index will Tell You What You Have and Where it Can be Found*

category (such as Book of Mormon; faith; psychology; etc.) at top left. List author, source, and date; then the entire quotation. These cards are kept alphabetically as to category, as are the details within the category as your file grows.

Small clippings may be pasted on the cards without rewriting, indicating only name and date of publication. These cards can be kept in a shoebox if you do not have a filecase.

2. FOLDERS and/or ENVELOPES for articles and clippings too large for cards. In this case, a reference card should be kept in the proper category of your card file. Put name of article, author, date, and publication from which it was taken, on the card. Also, add a few words to indicate the contents or conclusions of the article. For instance:

Faith (the category)

"We Walk by Faith" by John Doe, High Councilman & author.

Jan 1890 Instructor, page 216

(Shows how much our daily lives are lived by faith without thought of religion as such.)

3. BOUND COPIES OF THE CHURCH PUBLICATIONS such as the Era and Instructor. (Bound copies are specified because stacks of unbound magazines compose a very real fire hazard). If you wish to be really efficient, you should make index cards for each article in each magazine. Filed in the proper category, you will know at once that there is (for instance) an article on the Savior by James E. Talmage, page 820, Nov., 1961 Era. This takes very little time if it is done at once and consistently. It will never be done if you plan to do it every six months or once a year.

4. A BOX, BOXES, ENVELOPES, or whatever container necessary for the size and shape of the visual aids you wish to gather. Usually anyone teaching young children soon gets the habit of constantly watching for

pictures to clip and file. But don't forget that pictures are just as valuable for all age groups.

This will give you an idea of the possibilities. You can work out whatever best fits your situation. The important thing is that you feel the need of accumulating, and form the habit of recognizing useful enrichment materials, and of gathering them from every available source. If you have read through your entire course ahead of time, you will know what you are going to need. Also, you will recognize useful material you find in other reading.

SEVEN BASIC STEPS IN PREPARATION

Fig. 48

The following steps may seem to overlap other material mentioned, but they are a useful pattern for lesson planning.

Step 1. The first question to be answered by the teacher as he begins to prepare his lesson is: How best can I prepare the minds of my students to receive this lesson? Or, how can I set their minds going in the direction of the lesson? For example, suppose you were to teach a lesson on baptism as a basic principle of the gospel. If the lesson was for a group of 9-10 year olds, you might start by asking them to remember some of the reasons it was necessary for them to be baptized. If it was for a group of older students, you might start by asking how many were converts. Those who were could be asked if they had been baptized previously and in what manner. Either of these approaches could lead naturally into your discussion.

Step 2. Decide what you want the class to "take home", not six things or a dozen, but one main thought. This can be your lesson objective, whether or not it is the one you have made known to the class. All the discussion and smaller concepts should lead directly to this main idea or thought. When the class is over you want every member to leave feeling this was a lesson about such and such, to be able to put a name to it. For instance, in the lesson on baptism as a basic principle of the gospel, all of your stories, examples, and discussions should tend to prove that we have been given precise instructions by the Lord that baptism by immersion by someone having authority from Him is a necessary prerequisite to entering the Celestial Kingdom.

Step 3. The third step in the preparation of a lesson is to get the content of the lesson well in mind. An old farm hand with a reputation of being a philosopher, made this comment when asked to give his view on the importance of knowing and understanding lesson materials: "You can no more give what you ain't learned, than you can go back to where you ain't been." We need to study our materials well.

Most of the time our lesson materials cover much more than we could possibly use in a single class period. Much of what is contained in our outlines is meant to enrich the teacher and his understanding. It is the teacher's responsibility to be selective in choosing the central idea of the lesson and then developing it according to the needs of the specific group. As guides in selecting the material, the instructor must first consider two things, the lesson objective and the class. Whatever does not help to bring out the main thought of the lesson should be dropped from consideration. Then too, it may be that some materials which would help bring out the thought, would be too simple or too complicated for the particular class being taught. In this case it should be altered to meet student needs, or be left out altogether.

When the material to be used in developing the lesson is in narrative form, or is problem solving, our task is comparatively easy. When it is a body of history or facts, the task of relating those facts to student needs is much more difficult. In either event, the material must be mastered and made meaningful to students. When we are dealing with young and immature minds, the material we present needs to be concrete, and given so that there is no question as to where we stand or how we feel. That is, never end a class on a speculative note or with a question dangling, leaving students to try to decide where the Church stands. For example, in one class, a convert of only a year or two tentatively remarked that he wondered if it really made any difference to which church one belonged if he was a 'good person'. Rather than "start an argument", the teacher said he let it pass. A week or so later, the convert made the same remark, only this time it was not a question it was a positive statement. Again it was allowed to pass without correction or discussion. Within two months this person had left the Church, returning to the church of his family.

Sometimes a teacher does not know how to answer a question on a point of doctrine; or how to cope with a remark which he knows is wrong but can't explain exactly why in order to refute it. In the first situation he may say, "I'll check to make sure and tell you next class period." Then, he must be sure to find the answer and bring it out at the beginning of the next class. Wherever possible, send the inquiring student on a "field trip to the scriptures" and have him report his findings. In the second situation he might say, "That may be correct, but as I recall, the Church says so and so."

Step 4. The fourth step suggests that the teacher ask himself how best to apply the lesson to the lives of his students. The general aim of every lesson should be to change or modify (for the better) the conduct of those we teach. But every lesson also presents the specific question of how to modify conduct by the application of the particular idea developed in that lesson.

To illustrate, suppose you were teaching a group of boys and your subject was clean language. Your objective might be to show them there is no need for profanity and vulgar language. A week before presenting this lesson you could ask the class to keep track of how many times they heard a vulgar or profane word used. They might be given the assignment of making a mental list of these words every day for a week to get an idea for themselves how people's speech habits affect their lives. This awareness would help them as the class tried to analyze common vulgar expressions and why they are used. With this background of information, a further discussion could be developed around the idea (for example) of giving suggestions for alternatives; and on what one could do to help a friend break the habit of using profanity. Of course, this method of teaching must involve a knowledge of the group and their special problems. Generally, when we know our class well, their home environments and the community in which they live, we will have many useful clues on how to apply our lessons.

Step 5. The fifth step is to arrange the lesson materials and ideas on how to approach the lesson, into some kind of logical order. Again, there is no "one way" of accomplishing this. The important thing is to "find a plan that works, and then work that plan, as mentioned in Chapter IV. Even when one has found a successful plan, it is important to vary it for different lessons as the objectives lend themselves to different development. Let us look at a sample outline on the subject of how lesson materials might be arranged to help the teacher better prepare.

A SAMPLE LESSON PLAN ON LESSON PLANNING

Objective: To show the need for teacher preparation.

Attitude: The most important aspect of a teacher's work is his private preparation, wholly invisible to the eyes of the student.

Organization of Content	**Method**
I. The need of teacher preparation	
A. From the Scriptures	
B. From the lesson manual	
C. From other related writings	
D. Personal experience	
E. Prayer	
II. The organization of the lesson	
A. State the objective	1. What is your goal?
	2. What determines if it is appropriate?
B. List all pertinent ideas	1. Read
	2. Think
	3. Observe
	4. Converse

C. Build a brief or outline	1. Example to be placed on board.
	2. Or give to students in hand-out form.
D. Search for attractive illustrations	1. Visual aids (what will they be?)
	2. Stories
	3. Experiences
	4. Objects
E. Select an appropriate teaching procedure.	1. Short explanations by teacher to present problem
	2. Discussion—pro and con
	3. Illustrations
	4. C o n c l u s i o n s (To be drawn)

Step 6. Summarize. Conclusions are as important to a lesson as are the beginnings or the discussions. A successful conclusion is to a lesson what a safe landing is to an airplane flight. Again, there is no one formula that should apply, but one of the best is to summarize. Frequently it is necessary to present many thoughts in developing the one main idea. In doing so, it is easy for class members to become confused or to lose sight of the original goal. It is necessary to draw these points together in order to pinpoint the aim or purpose. After class each member might well ask himself "What have I learned today that I didn't know before?" and "How will this experience help me in solving my problems?" Let the teacher ask himself, "Did the lessons presented give the class new insight and the ability to meet life realistically? If not, could it be called a successful lesson?"

Step 7. Pray for the guidance and assurance of the Holy Ghost. Our Church leaders often remind us that the Lord helps those who try to help themselves. Or, as the old farmer told his hired hand: "Pray like it was up to the Lord to do it all, then work like it was up to you." Generally, there are three kinds of teachers in the Church, using preparation and non-preparation as the basis of classification: One group prepares without any thought of divine guidance. Another group leaves everything to the Lord (which usually means reliance on the impulse of the moment and it is frequently mistaken for inspiration). The third group (the one which should be our example) shows proper attitude in lesson planning, that of seeking divine aid in the early stages of preparation; then doing its utmost to think out the lesson with a mind open to the training experience gained in all previous fields of endeavor. We must remember that the Lord can inspire us in our initial studies and preparation as well as when we finally stand before our classes. The key thought lies in the scripture which tells us that the "Holy Ghost will bring all things to our *remembrance*" of which we have need. But first we must have something to remember, in other words, we need to put some money in the bank before we start writing checks!

With this thought in mind, we can say that the keynote of every teacher should be: prepare carefully, organize time and material well, use the light of human understanding, reason, and experience, and supplement them all with the inspiration of the Holy Spirit.

POINTS TO REMEMBER:

1. Two basic rules of teaching are preparation and organization.

2. Preparation includes a thorough knowledge of the entire course.

3. Organization includes a systematic program of gathering enrichment materials and keeping them available.

4. There are seven basic steps in the preparation of a lesson:

   A. Decide how to prepare student's minds to be receptive.

   B. Decide the main thought for the class to "take home".

   C. Get the lesson content well in mind.

   D. Decide how to apply the lesson to the lives of the lives of the students.

   E. Arrange ideas and materials in logical sequence.

   F. Summarize to pinpoint the main idea.

   G. Seek divine guidance early and constantly.

CHAPTER VII

Don't Forget You!

Even in the gospel-centered class YOU are a vital part of your lesson. To prove how vital, we need to discuss "you" from a different viewpoint; one which the average teacher seems to overlook. Years of teaching in the specialized field of our Church speech program, as well as in the auxiliaries, has proved two things of which teachers and speakers seem to be unaware.

1. When you teach you speak, and when you speak you teach. Speaking is such an integral part of teaching that every rule applying to good speaking, applies equally well to good teaching. And whenever you speak, you cannot avoid teaching.

2. When you stand before a group, your voice, words, looks, and actions combine to make a total effect upon those before you.

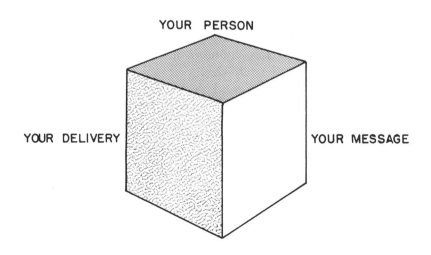

Fig. 49   *A Speech is a Cube*

During those teaching years, one illustration was developed which graphically demonstrates the two points stated above. This was "A speech is a cube." Since a good lesson and a good speech are so alike, we could say that a lesson also is like a cube, and demonstrate on that basis.

We are familiar with the fact that a lesson has three parts or "sides": an introduction, a body, and a conclusion. These are the three sides on which the teacher concentrates. But a lesson has three other sides of equal importance. These three, combined with the introduction, body, and conclusion, make six sides, and an object having six sides is a cube. If you examine a cube of any size, you will discover that regardless of which way you hold it, you can see only three of its six sides at any one time. So it is with a lesson. While the teacher is "seeing" the introduction, the body, and the conclusion (because this was his preparation) the group is "seeing" three entirely different sides. These three sides can be stated thus:

1. What you say: your message.
2. How you say it: your words and your delivery.
3. How you look and act while you are saying it: your clothing, your posture, your expression.

At first thought, it would seem that number one, "Your message," would be the most important. But if you will analyze all three, you will find that what you say can be completely nullified by how you say it, and how you look and act while you are saying it. Therefore, let us reverse the order and start our discussion with number three.

HOW YOU LOOK AND ACT WHILE YOU ARE SAYING IT: your clothing, your posture, your expression

The thing you may fail to remember is that the group *sees* you before it *hears* you. This means that clothing, jewelry, posture, and expression must be considered. The idea is to make a pleasant, but undistracting picture. That is, not to let the things they see interfere with the message they are to hear.

In the matter of clothing, a teacher should not wear vivid colors, patterns, or contrasts. For instance, a flaming red rose

Fig: 50

Don't Over-dress

on the shoulder of a simple gray wool dress is very chic. But the eye-catching quality of the vivid contrast of the red on the gray is distracting to the group and may keep them from concentrating on your message. This is true of the bright red or vividly patterned tie worn by a man (or a red shirt). Keep your clothing simple, neat and unobtrusive. I remember a woman from a political organization who came to speak to a college class studying American Institutions. Her dress was a simple tailored silk, but the material was done in multi-colored serpentine stripes about half an inch wide. The colors were not vivid, but every time she moved the stripes undulated like pastel snakes lined up for a race. I was so hypnotized by the shimmering movement of the dress that I completely missed her message. (But I can still see that dress!)

For the same reasons of distraction, jewelry should not be the dangling nor the flashing type. Movement catches the eye and is hard to ignore. This is not to say that women should not wear costume jewelry; it does mean to consider carefully all that you wear when you are teaching, speaking, or conducting a meeting. For example, the author has a penchant for wearing large and unusual earrings. But if she is to teach or speak she is careful to choose earrings that blend with her costume so that they will not catch the eye to the point of distracting the class.

This same element of distraction is found in the use of the hands, "playing" with things on the desk or pulpit. A man will often jingle coins or keys in his pocket. Both men and women are prone to twiddle with a pencil, their glasses, or the books and papers before them. All of these things distract and therefore detract.

Even the makeup a woman wears must be considered. Too much makeup on the face of a teacher is like the wrong frame on a picture. When the frame forces itself on your attention,

Fig: 51   *Too Much Make-up on a Teacher is Like the*
Wrong Frame on a Picture

it does so to the detriment of the picture. Just so when a woman's makeup is overdone, and therefore obvious, the effect for which she is striving is lost. Makeup is a part of good grooming. It should go without saying that both men and women teaching in the Church should be neat, clean, and well groomed regardless of either the humbleness or the high level of their economic status.

Another part of the pleasing picture for which you should strive is your posture. As you take your place at the front of the classroom, lift your chest so that your head will be up and your shoulders back. (Remember what Giblen said about what slumped shoulders and droopy head says about you.) Don't stand still like a soldier at attention, but comfortably erect, so that you look and will act, like the leader you are supposed to be. As you sit or stand erect, you will find that your mind is more alert. This applies to your students as well, for any audience tends to do what you do. If you are relaxed, they will be relaxed. If you slump, they will slump, physically and mentally. If you are stiff and ill at ease, they will become uncomfortable along with you and will not listen to what you are saying.

That same tendency is the big reason it is important to *smile*. Not only will it make the picture more pleasing to the eye, but your group will find it difficult not to smile back. Besides, it is hard to stay tensed when you are smiling, so smiling is the best way to ease your own nervousness. Therefore, before you say a word, as soon as you take your position, pause, look at your class and SMILE! Only then is it permissible to look down and arrange your papers, books and so forth. Nothing has ever seemed so cold and unfriendly as the speaker or the teacher who takes his position, looking only at the floor or his books; arranges papers, chalkboard, etc., etc., to his satisfaction and only then deigns to take notice that there are human beings waiting in front of him. This sets up a faint resentment or antagonism in the average person, which then must be overcome by the teacher before he can establish a friendly bridge for communication. The pause and the smile will relax both you and the group and set up a more receptive relationship.

One further point of what we might call classroom etiquette: the wearing of hats, coats, gloves, and ties. In the Church of Jesus Christ of Latter-day Saints it is the custom that neither men nor women wear hats when they are "up front" in any capacity. LDS women do not wear hats or gloves when teaching, speaking, or sitting on the stand. Yet it is not uncommon to see members doing all of these things. All of us have seen men without coats or ties praying, speaking, teaching, and conducting. All of us have seen women in the same situations *wearing* coats or hats or gloves. For both men and women it is equally bad taste, or if you will, bad manners. A man's suit coat is an integral part of his clothing and should be worn when participating in Church. A woman's coat has the same function as a man's topcoat and should be removed unless one is sitting in the audience. For Church leaders, and teachers are surely leaders, should uphold the dignity of the Church at all times. This does not mean long-faced solemnity, nor stiff unfriendliness. It does mean that if leaders would maintain the dignity of leadership in their looks and actions there would be less irreverence in our classes and our meetings. Respect for a teacher does not come with the title, it must be earned. If you show your lack of respect for the Church and your position in it by sloppy dress, posture, and actions, how can you build respect (either for yourself or the Church) in the members of your class?

All of this is not to say that the teacher should appear perennially in black or severe and unadorned clothing, acting like a monk in a TV show. It is to say be aware! Be aware that you are seen as well as heard. Dress and act more conservatively than you would on a more informal or festive occasion. In essence, you and your clothing may be compared to the cabinet which houses your grand piano: It may be very beautiful and expensive, it is rarely ornate. It is simple and dignified looking. It has a very useful and necessary function, but it never gets in the way of the music.

And this leads us to point two, the second side of the "cube" as the group sees it.

HOW YOU SAY IT: your words and your delivery.

Even more than your appearance, your words, your actions, and your tone of voice can nullify your message.

Fig. 52

Don't Over-do Your Message

1. *Don't begin with an apology!*

This is the big pitfall for the timid and the nervous, but most of all for the unprepared. Some even feel it is a sign of humility or modesty. It is much rather a sign of vanity! What, exactly, does the teacher hope to accomplish with his apology? Does he want the group to feel sorry for him? Or think he is noble for trying? Does he expect an apology will make them more tolerant of his lack of preparation? Is he inferring that only his personal comfort is important?

On very rare occasions it is necessary to offer an explanation. Usually it is not a good idea to try. As the sage said, "Your friends won't need it and your enemies won't accept it." Actually, the only thing an apology accomplishes is to embarrass the audience and make them uncomfortable. And when they are uncomfortable they won't like you and therefore won't listen.

Most times the group will not be aware of your nervousness, especially if you have something to say. Sometimes they may be unaware that you have not prepared as you had planned. But once you have told them, then your mistakes will be more glaring. If you are self-conscious, you are conscious of the wrong person—be more conscious of the group and the message you have for them. Simply do the best you can, whatever the circumstances, and start right in with your introduction. To start with an apology not only wastes time and embarrasses people, it weakens everything else you have to say.

2. *Be Alive!*

Enthusiasm is catching! If you can't work up any enthusiasm about your message, how can you interest others? To paraphrase the sage, you cannot light the fire (of enthusiasm) in someone else unless you have the spark within yourself. Fill yourself so full of the gospel and the joy of living it that it bubbles over. Or as the old preacher put it, "First I read's myself full, then I thinks myself straight, then I prays myself hot, and I let's myself go!"

Vary your tempo, change your pace frequently, raise and lower your voice. Be animated enough to seem alive, but don't overdo it. There was a boy in a Speech competition once who had a tendency to lean on the pulpit and stay in that position during his entire talk. His coach urged him to move around a little, to shift his position occasionally, even to step to one side or the other; in other words she tried to unfreeze him from the pulpit. On the night of the competition, the boy's nervousness and desire to win, combined to make him overdo the instructions. He paced up and down like a tiger in a cage. Needless to say, one extreme is as bad as the other.

Don't move around or gesture just for the sake of the gesture, do it as a natural result of feeling what you are saying. Don't worry about what you are going to do with your hands and feet, just *feel* the emotion and you will do the natural thing.

If you are the quiet, retiring type, you needn't try to make yourself into a breezy "jack-in-the box." You *can* practice being a little more animated. You *can* change your tempo or pace occasionally. You *can* change the pitch and tone of your voice sometimes. Don't try to imitate someone else, develop your own style, be yourself. But practice adding a little more animation and soon you will find yourself enjoying your teaching more than before. If enthusiasm is catching, with a little practice you can catch it yourself!

3. *Be aware of the tone you use.*

Habitually using the wrong tone creates more antagonism and misunderstanding between people than almost anything imaginable. This is to say that our tones cause reactions in those who hear. These reactions are either friendly or antagonistic, warm or cold. What we give comes back to us immediately like light waves bounced off a mirror. But the sad part is that we are, so often, unaware that our words and our tones are speaking different languages. We think if we mouth the proper words that is all that is necessary, forgetting that our tone is saying what we really feel. Think back, haven't you had someone say on being introduced "I'm happy to meet you," when his tone was clearly saying "Actually I'm bored to death?"

Lack of sincerity shows first and most plainly in the voice. You cannot convince anyone, especially a young person, that his salvation or welfare is important to you unless your tone of voice matches the warmth and love of your words. But it is in our homes that we find some of the most obvious demonstrations of this "common double talk."

You husbands, remember the last time you reached for the hammer you were sure you had left in its proper niche on the wall? When you asked your wife or one of the children "Where is the hammer?", what did your tone say? Did your tone leave it the simple question that it is? Or did your tone say "You-stupid-jerks-that-never-put-anything-back-where-you-got-it—WHERE'S MY HAMMER???" And when you received an answer was it, for example, "The hammer is on the bench in the garage," a simple statement of fact. Or on a rising inflection of anger at what was expressed in *your* voice, did the answer come back "It's right on the bench in the garage you dope, as anyone could see if he'd use his eyes instead of yelling his head off."

Our voices express what we really are and what we are really thinking. Therefore, one must become aware of the reality of this fact and its effect on others. Furthermore, we must deliberately practice improving our tones to express the warmth and love that, as Church teachers, we should feel toward our fellow men. This means deliberately cultivating that feeling of warmth and love, for as Garff takes a whole chapter to tell us "You speak what you are." If changes are necessary, they must come from within: changes in attitudes and in feeling. This is not something that can be turned on and off like an electric light, it is an expression of inner feeling. And it will express that feeling whether or no.

A shy or timid youngster, or one with a feeling of inadequacy, needs love and approval from a teacher. If that teacher voices impatience or irritation in his tone, that child can be discouraged completely from any class participation. So cultivate a feeling of warm, loving regard for your students. Then, let it be expressed in your tone as well as your words and actions.

4. *A word about enunciation, grammar, and diction.*

Many of us mumble our words as though we had a mouthful of marbles. The reason is, so many of us suffer from what Garff calls the "Three Most Common Faults" among speaking Americans:

Lazy lips; idle tongue; and immovable jaw.

All three of these can be overcome with a little awareness, and a little practice. The mouth cavity is the final resonance mixing chamber. That is where the tones are magnified and the voice becomes individual.

Our *lips* are a natural megaphone. When we use them, they help us to project our voices. But too many people move their lips about as much as a bunch of convicts in a TV show. Practice overdoing the sounds of B and P—make them explode from your lips. Do this two minutes a day for a few weeks and you will be surprised how flexible your lips will become. Becoming aware of the need for using your lips is half the battle.

For an *idle tongue*, try rolling your "R's," especially on words that start with "br." Here's a useful sentence to practice: "The brilliant, but brawny, young Bronchiologist, brawled before breakfast." Say that a dozen times a day, rolling your R's and you will soon have a flexible tongue.

For the *immovable* jaw, try singing Naw, Naw, Naw, up and down the scale. For the "N" the teeth are closed, for the "aw", the jaw is open at least two fingers wide. Two or three minutes of that a day will loosen up the jaw so that it can work as it was meant to do. Do these exercises when you are washing dishes, showering and shaving, ironing, or any time your hands are busy and your mind is free. They will add much to the clarity of your enunciation.

Of course, there is no substitute for actually pronouncing all the syllables of a word. Many of us have the bad habit of telescoping words, leaving out syllables, and slurring others. We are like the old man we met in Florida who called San Francisco "San Frisco." When asked why, he answered "O I dunno, too much trouble t'put in all them sylbls uhguess."

Diction also has to do with enunciation, but its more important definition (as found in Merriam-Webster) is "Use of the right word in the right place to express the idea." Mark Twain once said that the use of the right word and the almost right word was the difference between lightning and the lightning bug.

This thought serves to point up what is probably the greatest fault in the average teacher or speaker: the use of general words instead of specific words. Specific words make our meaning so much more clear. In other words, never say a flower, if you are talking of a rose. Never just say a rose if you can add to the picture with an adjective or two: a pink rose, or a large pink rose, a fragrant pink rose; for you are trying to paint a picture in the minds of the hearers.

We think in pictures. When you say "a flower," I don't see the letters f, l, o, w, e, r. I see a flower, so if you are talking of a rose, I may see a violet unless you paint a better picture by telling me the flower is a rose. A teacher is not effective until he has painted a picture with words, in the minds of his students. It follows that we should use specific words for clarity, picture words to help paint the picture. Instead of saying a man *went* by, say he ran, he hurried, he limped—whatever fits the picture you want them to see. If you practice following this rule, you will find you are communicating to better advantage, and are therefore a more effective teacher.

A WORD ABOUT GRAMMAR

Fig. 53

How is Your Grammar?

It is not our intention to go into *grammar* as such, but to point out two or three errors which are becoming more and more widespread.

A. The use of plural nouns and pronouns with singular verbs and vice versa. For instance, two that are commonly heard in our classrooms and from our pulpits:

"We feel in our heart." "They will remember it all their life."

Your subject must agree in number with your verb:

We (plural) feel in our (plural) hearts.
They (plural) will remember it all their (plural) *lives*.
I (singular) feel in my (singular) *heart*.
I will remember it all *my* life.

The exceptions would be sentences using you and your, which are either singular or plural.

B. The use of the adverb badly, when you mean the adjective *bad*. This has become so prevalent, even among otherwise educated people, that it needs a determined effort to stamp it out.

You can *see* badly; *hear* badly; and you *can feel* badly if you mean your fingers are numb. But *if you are ill* you feel *bad*. It is an adjective like glad, or sad, or mad. You don't feel gladly, or sadly, or madly, so why say you feel badly?

C. Two other words deserve "dishonorable" mention:

1. Git for get, is becoming all too common. The word is gEt, it rhymes with let, and met, and set. The use of gIt is either carelessness or ignorance.

2. Irregardless: This was apparently started by a comedian who was trying to be funny. But he has been taken seriously by all too many adults. IR is a prefix, or beginning of a word, meaning not, non, or un. Example: irrational, meaning not rational. LESS is a suffix, or word ending, meaning without. Therefore, regard*less*, means without regard. There is no such word as irregardless, it is syllables without meaning, or as listed in Walsh's Handbook of English, "A barbarism, or word distortion."[1]

Latter-day Saints have the reputation of being a highly literate people. Let us do our bit toward stamping out these speaking errors which make us sound illiterate.

And now for the third side of our lesson "Cube" as it is seen by the group:

---

[1]Walsh, J. Martyn and Walsh, Anna Kathleen, *Plain English Handbook*, McCormick-Mathers Publishing Co. Inc., Wichita, Kansas: 1959.

WHAT YOU SAY: your message.

To the teacher "objective" and "message" are synonymous.

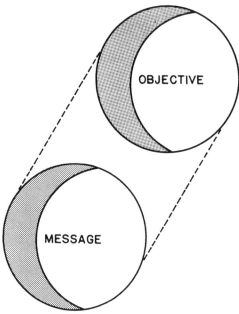

Fig. 54

To the Teacher — Objective and Message are Synonymous

It is the essence of your lesson that you want those who hear, to incorporate into their lives. This has been discussed in a previous chapter but let us discuss it briefly from this view:

1. Your subject as such will be provided by your lesson materials. But, let everything you add be pertinent to the time, place, age, size, and sex of the group. Cut out everything that is too general, that is, not specific enough to be valuable. For example, if you are teaching young people about having faith, don't generalize with statements like "All good people have faith." "Good" is too ambiguous, that is, it can be interpreted many ways. Therefore, the class will not know what you mean by "good" as you are using it. Nor will they know what "faith" has to do with your interpretation of "good." Your explanation must be simple enough, clear enough, and specific enough that the group can apply the concept to their own lives.

2. Keep to basic gospel topics and illustrations as much as possible. Use imagination to find a fresh approach, a new view of an old topic. For instance, at June conference a woman gave an impromptu talk on teaching young boys. She compared them to green apples: They had to be handled carefully or they would make you pucker up good, or even give you a stomach ache. But if they were prepared with love and care, boy what an apple pie they made!

All of us have imaginations—some of us need to cultivate them. For an imagination is a most useful tool for the teacher of any age group.

3. Time: Watch that clock. This problem is a complicated one for the teacher. If he doesn't have enough material prepared, he is apt to have a major discipline problem on his hands. However, if he runs out of time, usually it is at the expense of (A) the assignment for the next class period; (B) the proper concluding of the lesson being given; or (C) a proper dismissal of the group.

Normally, it is necessary for a teacher to prepare more material than he feels he can use. The reason is that it is impossible to foretell how much discussion will result from a given question. The most experienced teachers often miscalculate the time needed for various parts of a lesson, simply because it is not possible to judge exactly. This is one reason it is so important that your lesson plan include a timetable, and that you keep to it as far as possible. Having a timetable also helps a teacher to be flexible, and not get upset when discussion or lack of it upsets his timetable. Have you ever seen the agenda for a Sacrament Meeting or a Stake Conference meeting? The Bishop or Stake President must cope constantly with the speaker who goes overtime. With a look at his agenda he knows exactly where his program should be at any given time and makes his adjustments accordingly. Make yourself a timetable on your agenda to help you to leave one portion of your lesson and move to another at the proper time. Learn to do this without making the class feel that you never have time to listen to what they have to say.

In terms of our lesson "cube," these are the points to remember about your message: Be sure all material and ideas are suitable to your group and to the occasion; keep to basic gospel ideas and illustrations to bring the gospel into their daily living; and have a timetable, keeping to it as far as possible.

YOUR EXAMPLE AND YOUR TESTIMONY

There are two other points about "you" which are of vital importance to your class. These points influence others whether you wish it or not. They are: Your example and your testimony. These are interdependent, because if you haven't a testimony of the gospel you may not feel the urgency of setting the proper example. Because they are so interdependent, they need to be discussed together for this chapter.

People of all ages need to associate with leaders they can respect. They need to feel their teachers have strength in their convictions—it gives comfort and security to the members of the group. They need someone to emulate, to inspire them to strengthen their own convictions. They need the example of such a leader to show them that they too can reach the goal.

Therefore, what you do outside of class is as important as what you do in it. The members of your class will be watching constantly to see if you DO the things you tell them to do. This applies not only to children, but to adults as well. Always, the weak in the faith look to the strong for inspiration. How many current Senior Aaronics became inactive because a leader (teacher) did not *live* the gospel? For instance, all of us may know someone who has never returned to the Church because the "leader" who was trying to reactivate him, used such foul language on the job where they both worked.

Remember the words of Alma to his wicked son Corianton? "O my son, how great iniquity ye brought upon the Zoramites; for when they saw your conduct they would not believe my words."[1] Let us paraphrase that: "O my teacher, how great

---

[1] Alma 39:11, *Book of Mormon.*

Fig. 55

Members of Your Class are Watching you Constantly

iniquity you have brought upon your class; for when they saw your conduct they would not believe your words."

As indicated in Chapter I, we cannot give our testimonies to others. But our example can accelerate or seriously hamper the efforts of others to find a testimony for themselves. The scriptures tell us that our reward will be great if we labor all the days of our lives and bring only one soul to God. What will be our punishment if our example turns *away* even one soul *from* God?[2]

POINTS TO REMEMBER:

1. You are seen before you are heard.
2. Let your clothing, jewelry, posture, and expression combine to make a pleasing, but unobtrusive picture.
3. Be alive—use voice, body, and enthusiasm to add to your message.

---

[2]Part of the material in this Chapter is taken from a booklet compiled by Cherie B. Parker called, *Prayer and Conducting Tips.* While this booklet is still available from her, it is in the process of revision for publication later this year.

4. Let your tone express only warmth and friendliness.

5. Practice for better enunciation, diction, and grammar, that you may "paint a better picture" in the minds of your students.

6. Be sure your message takes the gospel into the lives of your students.

7. Accelerate the growth of their testimonies by your own living of the gospel.

CHAPTER VIII

Ammunition For the Classroom

PART I

Loading Your Gun

Good methods are to teaching what ammunition is to the successful battle. The best bullets are valueless if they don't

Fig. 56

Good Methods are to Teaching what Ammunition is to the Successful Battle

fit your gun, or if they were designed to go 500 feet and your target is 1000 feet over the next hill. If the purpose of teaching is to help students to learn, then as teachers we must be concerned with how we can teach so that learning will actually take place. It is a fallacy to assume that any one teaching method can be used by all teachers to fit all class situations, any more than that one bullet would fit all guns. This is why no magic formula has been developed which will solve the problem of method selection. In general, there are six methods of teaching: question and answer, class discussion, lecture, project, story-telling, and role-playing. The use of visual aids is sometimes thought of as a method of teaching, but these "tools for teachers" are not so much a technique as they are aids or enrichment materials to be used with all methods.

With such a selection of methods available the teacher may well ask, "How do I know which one to use?" There is no general rule that can be given. In the average teaching

Fig. 57

Use a Variety of Methods

situation, no one method is best. In a given lesson, one teacher may use one method, while for the same lesson with the same age-group involved, another teacher may use an entirely different technique. Both of them *can* be equally successful, the question is whether or not learning took place.

FACTORS IN METHOD SELECTION

There are several factors that we need to keep in mind as we determine which technique might be best in a given instance. The first is the objective the course outline suggests,

Fig. 58

Aim at the Objective

or the aim the teacher has chosen for the lesson. For example, a lesson entitled, "Am I My Brother's Keeper" might have as its objective "To help students understand brotherhood as Jesus taught it in the New Testament." The teacher might want to spend the entire class period lecturing on what he has learned from the scriptures on the subject. Or, he might assign two or three students to tell brief stories about various persons in the Bible who understood the principle of brotherhood.

Another lesson on the same subject might have a different objective. It could be, "To help students discover how to serve their fellow men." This objective suggests the use of discussion or the question and answer method. The use of a thought provoking topic such as, "Is the giving of money alone a real way of serving one's fellow men?" could stimulate a very interesting discussion. This is not to say that the one technique is better than the other. However, it does point out that one method may put across a certain point better than another technique.

The second thing we need to take into consideration is the time element. The amount of time we have for a given lesson

Fig. 59
Time is an Important Element in Method Selection

helps to determine the method we select. Projects, class recitation, and role-playing take more time than the others. One of the advantages of the lecture method is the possibility of presenting large quantities of factual information in a brief period. However, the lecture method is seldom the most effective way to teach since individual participation is absent. Also, only a very interested and already motivated group will be able and willing to absorb large quantities of factual information. It should be remembered that the most effective teaching is experienced when individual class members take an active part. Consistent with what has been said in previous chapters, students learn best when they are personally "doing".

Third, the experiences and backgrounds of class members will often help to determine the method to be employed. For

Fig. 60
Backgrounds of Class Members help Determine Methods

example, a method using class participation such as a discussion, or a question and answer approach where different experiences of students could be brought out, would greatly enrich a lesson on "What it means to be a Latter-day Saint." Even then your questions would be different for a group of converts in a small branch, from the questions you would use in an area where life-time LDS predominated. Regardless of the lesson subject, any class participation method calls for an understanding of the group so that the teacher can draw on student experiences and fit the lesson to their backgrounds.

When asked which teaching method is the best, we can only reiterate that no one of them is best. Each method has its own place and purpose. Probably a combination of two or more methods in any given lesson is more nearly the ideal. For instance, a teacher might use the lecture method, or even a story, for the first ten minutes, to set up a situation for the problem-solving or discussion methods. In teaching, as in all of our experiences, variety is the spice that will keep the student coming back for more. A good rule of thumb is this: If your class members can predict with reasonable accuracy what you will be doing from week to week, you can be certain that you are **not** motivating students to learn. Remember, methods or techniques are not ends in themselves. They are only means to an end, and curiosity about what you are going to do next, or how "this" is going to fit the discussion, is an excellent motivating factor.

Regardless of the technique employed, the all important thing to remember is to teach the whole student, as Bennion suggests. Our very purpose for being in Church classes is to give our students a rich spiritual experience, and experiences involve the **whole** student.

STUDENT INVOLVEMENT IS VITAL
IN EVERY METHOD

Fig. 61

Student Involvement is Vital in every Method

We have already discussed the importance of involving each class member in the lessons we present. Also, it has been pointed out that if learning is to take place, it will require the learner to think. You might ask "How do you get a person to think?" The answer is, involve him. For rarely will an individual think unless he is confronted with a problem. Problem solving is vital in all methods of teaching, both in motivating people to think and getting them to discuss. Dr. Leonard Rice, in an outstanding article entitled "Earmarks of a Good Teacher", has said:

"Who wishes to motivate discussion will center attention of his class upon a problem which is real and vital. The intellectual activity of the class is then focused upon the problem in an attempt to solve it. Discussion follows automatically as each person in the class realizing that a solution is important, contributes his own experience and learning toward a common solution. Argument is out of place: a group of sincere people are sharing experiences, convictions, and information directed toward the mutual solution of a problem vital enough to deserve their attention".[1]

It would be one thing for the leader of a Parent and Youth class to pose a question like "How do we get children to go to Church"? It would be infinitely more interesting and profitable to say "My nine year-old has suddenly decided she doesn't want to go to Sunday School anymore. What can I do"? This is what Rice is saying above.

PITFALLS IN PROBLEM SOLVING USE

There are two major pitfalls to keep in mind when working up your "problems" for class discussions, either of which, if you fall into it, will defeat your purpose of motivating to learn. The first is, having a specific solution in your own mind and challenging the class to guess what it is. Someone might guess, but most of the class will be too bored or resentful to try. As Rice says, "It is well to keep in mind what a problem is. A problem, whatever else it may be, is something for which

---

[1]Rice, Leonard, *Earmarks of a Good Teacher.*

no solution exists at a given time and place. As soon as a solution is found, a problem ceases to exist."[2]

This means that the teacher must keep an open mind and let various solutions be suggested, as they invariably will be if open discussion is allowed. For outside of mathematics,

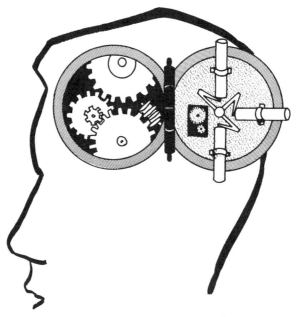

Fig. 62   *Keep an Open Mind*

where two and two can only make four, there are few problems which have only one solution. Each class member will find a solution from and in harmony with his own background. It is well for you to have a solution in your own mind and add it to the others when all who will, have expressed themselves. But do not put it forward as the only solution, refusing to accept or consider others thought out by the class.

The second pitfall is asking the type of question which is open to a simple factual answer. Frequently one can observe a teacher asking a question that he obviously expects will bring forth a good deal of discussion, only to have one informed person answer it in a few well-chosen words. For instance, a

[2]Ibid.

teacher might say, "We know that Jacob stole Esau's blessing, but why was it only Esau's blessing"? This would provoke no discussion at all if one person said "Because he was the oldest". If the teacher had said "We know that Jacob stole Esau's blessing, but why did Jacob feel it was necessary, and justified? And do you agree?" considerable discussion could be provoked. Furthermore, the discussion could clarify a much misunderstood episode in Bible history and gospel doctrine.

Questioning is an art, an art that is learned. There are many facets to its use. In general, we avoid questions which have brief, factual answers, unless we are testing rote memory as is discussed in Chapter XI. The most useful questions are those which set up a problem to be solved, which make students weigh and think, consider and conclude. This is learning.

Rice gives an interesting example of the contrast between a flat question and one which stimulates thinking and weighing. He says "Consider a question such as the following: 'How far should a Latter-day Saint go in avoiding the presence of evil?' This question states an important problem, but a teacher putting it to a class is likely to be disappointed by getting little response. Now what can we do to make this 'presence of evil' question come alive for a group? (how about) The best place to get re-enforced cardboard boxes is in a liquor store; should I as a Latter-day Saint and a teacher of young people enter a liquor store to buy, not liquor, but cardboard boxes? Members of the class will literally jump into discussion of this problem made objective by such a case. Their minds will explore all the possible results of the behavior suggested and each person will contribute his views".[3]

In working with these problem-solving, here-and-now-situation discussions, the teacher will not know ahead of time just what the class will decide is the best solution. He must guide and control the discussion without stifling it. In other words, let them quest back and forth as they explore the possibilities, but keep them considering the main point. They can get far afield exploring tangents. The teacher needs to bring them back to the main road, but never force them to a specific destination or solution.

The important thing to remember in using problem-solving in the technique selected, is that the thinking mind moves from the particular to the general. However, valid generalizations are not possible, nor are people much interested in generalizing until and unless they know specific facts and situations, that is, cases from which to generalize. In other words, we can't make a point by generalizing. We make points by being specific, working with specific situations or cases.

Further, it should be pointed out that problem-solving and here-and-now situations can be adapted to every method a teacher might choose in his lesson approach. If the problem or situation selected is realistic and within the range of student experience and the teacher has included the basic steps of learning (exposure, repetition, understanding, conviction, and application) it is reasonable to assume that the learning they have achieved in class will be transferred into everyday life.

3Ibid.

PART II

On the Firing Line

Having considered the factors in method selection and the necessity of involving students in whatever technique is used, let us now consider how the various kinds of methods may be employed.

QUESTION AND ANSWER METHOD

It was Kipling who wrote:

"I have six honest serving men;
They taught me all I know;
Their names are 'what' and 'why' and 'when'
And 'who' and 'where' and 'how' ".

Use these honest serving men in formulating your questions; for questions which are carefully prepared and properly used, can be an important factor in the learning process. They can be used for many purposes, eight of which are listed below:

1. To open a discussion.
2. To arouse interest.
3. To cause thinking.
4. To develop subject matter.
5. To get individual participation.
6. To control and direct discussion.
7. To drill.
8. To test understanding.

These are the characteristics of a good question which teachers need to keep in mind: First, it should stimulate thought. Second, it should draw forth a comprehensive answer, rather than a simple yes or no. Third, it should be adapted to the experience of the student to whom it is directed.

Through planning and practice, the teacher can develop the ability to think clearly and rapidly. This is important if the question and answer method is to be effective. Also, he should practice *wording* questions, so that he accomplishes his purpose when inviting a response. There is a tendency on the part of many teachers to use only one type of question. This often leads to little or no discussion among the group. More

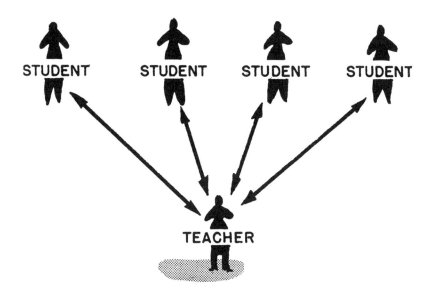

Fig. 63

Question and Answer

often than not, the use of only one type of question creates an attitude of indifference in people. Teachers would do well to consider the following chart which shows several types of questions, what they do, and how they can be constructed. (See page No. 149 for chart).

Since most Church teachers are not trained in the art of questioning, it may be helpful to keep in mind these three thoughts, when you are planning a lesson which involves questions:

1. **Questions need to be planned in advance.** If the teacher is not in the habit of using questions regularly, then while the lesson plan is being constructed, the questions should be worked out so that the desired student response can be brought about.

2. **Questions should be brief and to the point.**

3. **Questions should be so worded that their meanings are clear and understandable;** keeping in mind the age-level and experience of the group.

Type of Question	Description	Example
1. Classify (group)	Tell what kinds — Illustrate — Show how — give example.	The Lord has said, "Honor your parents." Can you give some examples of things we would do if we carried out this commandment?
2. Compare (liken)	How are they alike or different? Interpret — In your opinion — Justify (defend) account for.	How can we compare the social conditions in the time of Christ with social conditions in our country today?
3. Criticize (judge)	What is good or bad — outline (sketch). Give main point of reason.	What is the value of the Ten Commandments today?
4. Define (limit)	Tell what it is. Review (recall) repeat.	What is meant by the word "ordinance?" Who can repeat the first article of faith and tell what it means?
5. Describe (picture)	How does it look? Summarize (reduce). Tell in a few words.	We have considered the many ways a church member might serve his country more effectively. John, will you summarize what the class has been saying up to this point?
6. Discuss (reason)	Talk about — tell something about.	Discuss the scriptural basis for tithing in the Book of Mormon. (III Nephi 24:7-12) (Alma 13:15)
7. Distinguish (contrast)	Which is different — Trace (follow) What are the steps?	Trace the development of the LDS Church Education program from 1832 to the present, and contrast the differences in philosophy with that of the Catholic parochial schools.
8. Explain (make clear)	Tell how — verify (prove). Is it true?	If a friend asks you how you know the Book of Mormon is true, what would you tell him?
9. Here-and-now situations (What to do)	Solve problems — What would you suggest? How would you help? Advise and counsel!	Suppose your best friend wanted to be married in the temple, but he was not eligible since his attitude and conduct were contrary to gospel teachings. How could you help him qualify?

Consistent with the philosophy of learning proposed in this book, teachers should avoid the over-use of factual questions. Instead, it is suggested that the teacher ask more questions involving the thought process. In this way, class members may be led to new and deeper insight which is the purpose of all our teaching.

CLASS DISCUSSION METHOD

The class discussion method is one of the most popular techniques used in teaching. It is also one of the most effective, since it often involves a large number of the group and tends to hold their interest. Regardless of the topic, people of all ages like to express themselves. The use of discussion gives each individual an opportunity to contribute his thoughts and experiences. A good discussion can make any subject much more meaningful, as well as more interesting. In a good discussion, attitudes are formed and decisions are made.

The class discussion method is a co-operative search for truth, seeking the solution to a common problem. No one

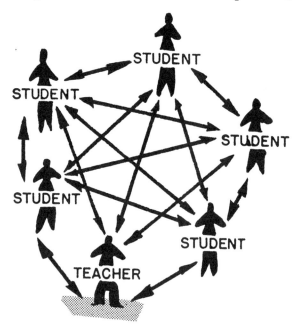

Fig. 64

Class Discussions

person, including the teacher, has all the answers. However, most probably, everyone in the class can shed *some* light on how the problem might be solved. This is why it is important for each class member to participate. It is equally important to (1) make certain that the problem you select to discuss is of major significance, and (2) it must be a problem about which there are honest differences of opinion.

For instance, a teenage class might be facing a problem like this: Many homes in the Church find it difficult to hold family prayers. The cooperation of each member of the family is needed if this vital counsel from the Lord is to be carried out in our homes. In posing this problem to your group you might ask this question, "What would you suggest in the following situations"?

Case number one: The High School age daughter of the family has been on the "outs" with her family for a couple of days. A very unpleasant situation has developed where harsh words have been exchanged between the girl and her parents. Restrictions have been placed on the daughter by the parents and the girl thinks she is being treated unfairly. In what ways can family prayer be of value in this situation?

Case number two: In this home, the family is on a split time schedule. The father has to be at work before any of the others are up. At noon time none of the family is home, each takes a lunch to school or work. By the time the evening meal is prepared most of the family are rushing to meet their many evening appointments. Let's have some suggestions as to how this family can meet the problem of holding family prayer.

Case number three: This is a family that prays together regularly. The parents are careful to see that the time set aside for family prayers is kept free. But the prayer itself has become stereo-typed and formalized. What suggestions can we offer which would make family prayer both more spiritual and more meaningful?

In structuring a discussion, there are certain prescribed steps which must be observed. These have been stated by John Dewey, as his outlined basic procedure used in problem-solving.

1. State the problem.
2. Define the problem.
3. Discuss the issues.
4. Identify the possible solutions.
5. Evaluate the possible solutions.
6. Make a decision.
7. Act — if action is needed.

All of the above steps can be used in the lesson outline and become a natural part of the class discussion. As the problem is stated and defined, the teacher (or class member) can list the issues and possible solutions on the board as questions are raised. Whatever the problem, the important thing to remember in conducting any discussion is that a *decision must be reached*. Whether or not any action should follow, will depend on the problem under discussion.

The teacher has a further responsibility when he leads a discussion. It is vital that he be aware of the many pitfalls which can destroy the consideration of even the most pertinent problem. Here are some rules to keep in mind:

1. Encourage participation.
2. Allow freedom of expression.
3. Avoid monopoly — either by the class members or the teacher.
4. Keep the discussion on the track.
5. Avoid wasting time on issues that are unimportant.
6. See all sides of the discussion.
7. Summarize, reach a decision, and conclude.

LECTURE METHOD

The lecture method is one of the oldest techniques known to the teaching profession. For centuries the teacher was the only source of information in a classroom, which increased the emphasis on this approach. With the advent of books and printed materials, other teaching methods were soon developed; but over the years the lecture method has remained the traditional one.

The lecture method is probably the most widely used technique in Church classes, particularly with older groups. Yet it is the most difficult of all methods to use effectively, because there is no assurance that any learning will take place. Even though a class may appear to be attentive, because they are sitting quietly during a lecture, teachers should not confuse the lack of disturbance with learning. Quite often class members will sit quietly during a lecture because they do not want to be bothered or embarrassed by questions that might be raised. It has already been pointed out that if learning is to occur, class members need to engage in some kind of activity; either mental, physical, or emotional. The lecture method is effective only if these kinds of activities have been achieved.

This does not mean that lectures should not be used. On the contrary, the lecture has some distinct advantages over other methods. When the teacher uses a lecture, he can cover

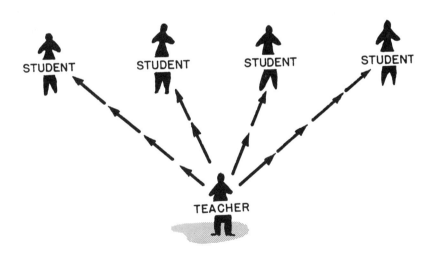

Fig. 65

Lecture

a vast amount of material in a relatively short time. Many times a teacher will have information which is not available to students, and the lecture is the fastest and most convenient way to give it to a group. In Church classes time is always a factor. If the teacher is to follow the many suggestions in this book (regarding the need for involving students in class activities such as a problem solving) then it is necessary to spend an occasional period covering the many facts which will give meaning and understanding to the subject matter.

Another real advantage of the lecture is the control it gives the teacher. Not only can he determine what information to give, but when to give it. One of the big limitations of most other methods is the temptation to get away from the subject and dwell on side issues that are not relevant. By controlling the subject matter with a lecture, the teacher can usually control the class as well. While lecturing does not guarantee student interest or motivation, it does have its place as one of the many methods that should be utilized. One example of the lecture might be when a teacher cites a personal experience in his lesson presentation.

The disadvantages of this method are many. Perhaps the greatest weakness is its failure to take into account the individual needs and differences of the group. When a teacher does not know what his students are thinking, there is always danger that effective learning will be absent. Teachers cannot tell by the way a person looks, whether or not learning is taking place. He must have responses, answers to questions, and comments made by the students in order to judge their understanding and growth.

It should be emphasized again that there is no one method that is best. The lecture approach has a place in teaching, but it would seem that a combination of many methods in each class period would make for greater interest, more participation, and better learning.

THE PROJECT METHOD

A project is any specifically assigned or planned activity in which class members engage to broaden their understanding of a principle, or to express learning they have achieved. The activity may take place in or out of the classroom. The project method is a very effective one since it gives students a chance to take the theory of the subject matter with which they are dealing and put it into practice by working out a problem. There are many gospel principles that cannot truly be learned

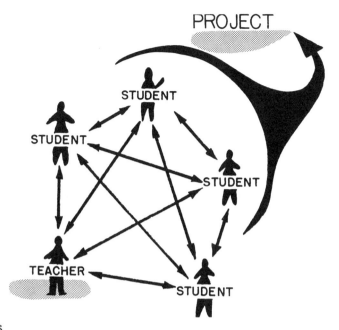

Fig. 66

Project

except by "doing." Remember, the closer learning is related to the direct experience, the greater the chances for learning to be transferred into individual lives.

All too frequently, classes in religion "talk about" gospel principles but do little if anything "with" them. It is not uncommon to sit in a class and discuss one of the Saviour's teachings at length, but seldom do those classes have the opportunity to "see how" such a principle works in life.

The purpose of the project method is to get class members to *experience* their religion as well as discuss it. For instance, if you were teaching a class of young people (any class from age 8-20) and your topic was service, you might have a class project of visiting a children's hospital. During such a trip the students could be given assignments (in addition to observing) to read to the children, or to present a program they had worked up for the occasion. Or they might make little gifts which could be used by a confined child.

The author recalls an experience with such a project involving an all-star athlete. At age eighteen this boy had never in his life done anything for anyone else just for the joy of serving. After reading bedtime stories for nearly forty minutes to a six year-old, whose little body was held in traction, he tearfully reported to his teacher, "I know now what the Savior means when He says . . . He who loses his life in the service of others . . . shall find it".

Another example involved a group of twelve year-olds who had a lesson on reverence. One Sunday morning they were asked, "How many of you would like to see a miracle performed?" Immediately, almost every hand shot into the air. The teacher quickly got the student's curiosity aroused by explaining that in order to perform one, every member of the class must be personally involved. He reminded them of the Ward's problem of maintaining reverence during Sunday School, and suggested that they could help solve this problem.

When he was told of the plan, the Bishop was delighted to have the help of the class, and by the next Sunday morning the students were prepared. Appropriate signs had been made by several of the students and were placed in the foyer as reminders. Other students were stationed at strategic points throughout the building to remind ward members to be reverent. Because of their personal interest, all class members were very willing to set a good example by being reverent themselves. Attention had been called to the class project by the Bishop, so that the class had ample opportunity to put its plan into action. This project lasted for one month. At the end of that time, the good results were so obvious that all the class felt well rewarded for their participation — and they were able to see that a "miracle" truly could be performed.

Committee activities, individual assignments, and panel discussions are other forms of the project method. While these activities do not always involve the students to the same extent as the examples above, they are excellent projects for getting class members to see problems, think them through, and suggest solutions.

For instance, an adult class might be considering the problem (prevalent both in and out of the Church) of the lack of interest in reading the scriptures. The teacher could begin by reading the following statement from William E. Berrett's book "Teachings of the Book of Mormon."

"A recent survey in a midwest college revealed that only some five per cent of the students could name a dozen books of the Bible, while there was an appalling lack of knowledge among nearly all students concerning the message that the Bible contained. Among Latter-day Saints there is a great neglect not only of the Bible but also of latter-day revelations as well. A survey of one thousand missionaries entering the mission home at Salt Lake City, preparatory to entering the mission field, revealed that one half of the number had never completely read the Book of Mormon and less than five per cent had read all of the Doctrine and Covenants."[4]

Reading this reference could set the stage for an active panel discussion. A group consisting of from four to six members could be brought forth to talk over this statement. Half of the panel members could be given the assignment of defending the negative position that:

1. The scriptures have no modern-day value.
2. The scriptures are meaningless in terms of our immediate problems.
3. Our modern society has outgrown the message of the scriptures.

The other half of the panel members could then defend the positive aspects of the problem:

1. The scriptures do have modern-day value. (Evidence could be cited).
2. The scriptures are filled with meaning for modern-day problems.
3. The message of scripture is universal and timeless in its value; God's word and truth are always relevant, regardless of the passing of time.

---

[4]Berrett, Wm. E., *"Teachings of the Book of Mormon";* Deseret Book Company.

At the conclusion of the discussion, a summary of the values of the scriptures could be listed on the board. And perhaps a "mental field trip" into the scriptures by the whole class would help show evidence of their importance.

ROLE PLAYING AS A METHOD

The role playing method of teaching is simply giving class members the opportunity to put themselves into various situations in such a way that they live them vicariously. Some

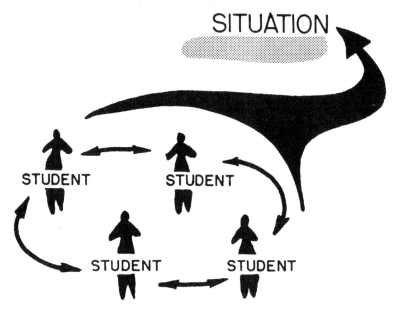

Fig. 67

Role Playing

of these situations could be imagined to let students see how they would react in a real experience. Others could be reenactments of things they themselves had done; while still others might be presentations or modern-day happenings of factual importance.

The role playing method is very effective since it is so natural to all of us. It might be said that there is a little of the actor in all of us, from the cradle up. Watch any child imitate his parents, brothers and sisters, or movie and television personalities, and you will see role playing in effect. Although we might not physically play the roles, it is normal for all of us to put ourselves in the places of others in all types of circumstances, thus going through situations we might not otherwise experience.

In the classroom these normal human tendencies can be well utilized to help students learn specific principles. For example, the lesson objective for a class of nine year-old girls in Primary, was to teach that we use good prayer language to show respect for our Heavenly Father. Since the abstract term "respect" was a difficult concept for them to understand, the teacher gave them here-and-now situations in the form of role playing. She had them act out three skits about attitudes of respect which they already understood, first doing the wrong thing and then doing the correct thing.

The first skit showed a young girl racing to get the only seat available in the bus (or the room), before an older woman could reach it. Then the two girls acted out what should have have been done, one being the girl and the other the woman.

The next showed a girl being very disrespectful to her mother by talking back. Then the girls reversed the scene and played the correct actions. In the third skit, two more girls showed first the wrong procedure, then the correct way to meet a queen, by curtsying low to Her Majesty, in the traditional way.

Because the girls were familiar with these situations, either from personal experience or natural interest, they enjoyed depicting the wrong attitudes; and they knew without any help from the teacher, how to present the correct ones. This understanding of respect helped the girls to a greater desire to respect their Heavenly Father.

If your class is an older group, the role playing would be handled a little differently. An example would be to assign two of them to be parents, others to be members of the family. Then pose a problem (a good here-and-now situation) and have the "parents" decide how to handle it. There are few better ways to have a teenager (for instance) take a look at his own behavior and how it affects others.

STORY TELLING AS A METHOD

Abraham Lincoln once said the reason he told so many stories was that stories brought understanding more quickly. That is why story telling is one of the most useful methods of teaching. Like all the others, it doesn't "just happen naturally", it takes work and patience, knowledge and skill to use story telling effectively. But if we, as teachers, are willing to *give* the first two, almost any one of us can acquire the others.

A story can be used to introduce a lesson; as the body of a lesson; to sum up a lesson; or to illustrate one or more points of the lesson. Stories can be used to hold the interest of our

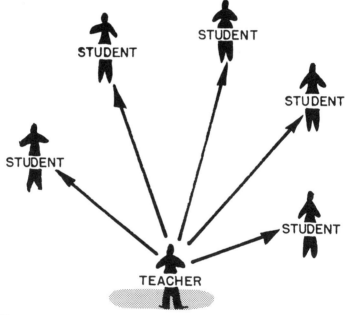

Fig. 68

Story Telling

students while we point out a gospel truth. They can be used to teach great attributes of character, as the faith of a Nephi or the courage of a Samuel. They can be used to bring understanding of the lands and customs of our ancestors, or of today's converts from foreign countries. Almost the only limit on the use of stories to enrich our lessons, is the limit of the teacher's resourcefulness and imagination.

HOW TO CHOOSE A STORY

Action is a prime requisite for a telling story. That is why many wonderful reading stories fall flat when someone memorizes or reads them aloud. Even when we are teaching attributes of character we do it by showing the attributes in action. For instance, in teaching of Lincoln's honesty, one could tell the story of his walking five miles to return a penny to a woman he found he had shortchanged at his grocery store.

A good telling story must have action, suspense, and a climax toward which to build. It should have only enough description to set the stage, to paint the picture as a backdrop for the action; but not enough to get in the way of the action. The group must follow the plot by listening only, so we can't afford to confuse them with too much description.

The story must be appropriate to the time, the place, and the age group involved. Stories of real people, like our pioneers, are more interesting than fictional stories. The lives of our pioneers tell us of *our* history, *our* ideals, *our* heritage. Therefore, we identify ourselves with them more easily, we share their experiences.

Obviously any story chosen for helping to teach the gospel, must be clean, wholesome, and moral. It need not always be a spiritual story, but a worthwhile story usually has a built-in moral that does not have to be pointed out. Never use a story just because it is interesting, useful, or "cute". If it doesn't lead toward your lesson objective, do not use it at all.

PREPARING THE STORY

Probably the most needed and least understood skill in preparing a story for telling is cutting it. Very rarely can a story be found that is just right in length, action, and material.

The first step is to read the story straight through. Then read it again, mentally stripping it of all but the basic action. Second, make an outline or list of the incidents in sequence. Cut out all the minor incidents and characters so as to build the main thread of the plot. Keep only those characters and incidents which are necessary to the main plot so that it will be easy to follow. This is the time to cut all unnecessary description for the same reason: to make the plot easy for the listener to follow. In other words, cut everything that does not *advance the plot*, no matter how interesting, true, or colorful it may be.

The third step is to put what is left into your own words. Retain bits of dialogue and phrasing that lend color or sometimes dignity to the story. For example, using the actual words of Christ often lends weight and majesty where it is needed. In Bible stories use an occasional word or phrase for color as ". . . the shepherds *abiding* in the fields."

Always the language you use should fit the age level of your group. Keep away from long or complicated words which will act as stop-lights in the minds of your listeners. Put most of the conversation in your own words too. For instance, "Johnny", said the Mother, "finish your chores and get ready for supper", would become "The mother told Johnny to finish his chores and get ready for supper." Occasionally use the actual dialogue of the author if it improves the "picture" or helps the plot.

Fourth, do not memorize either the original story or the cut version you have made. A story is not a dramatic reading, or a play in which you actually become the characters. It is a shared experience: you, the author, and the listeners. So read and reread your outline until you have the events clearly in your mind, then tell it aloud to your mirror and time yourself carefully. Reread and retell it several times, but make no attempt to use the same words — memorize only the events in sequence.

We have our voices, our hands and bodies, and our expressions to help us tell the story. Consequently it will take fewer words than were on the printed page. Only if you tell the story mostly in your own words will it sound spontaneous; for "telling" words and "writing" words are quite different. That is why it is so easy to spot the story or the talk that has been memorized, no matter how well it has been done.

THE PARTS OF THE STORY

As you cut and outline and put into your own words, remember that a story is like a lesson or a speech in that it has the same three parts: An introduction, a body, and a conclusion.

The introduction sets the stage. It tells the listeners the where, when, who, and a hint of the "what" to stimulate their interest. To illustrate, let me tell you the way I begin a story that I frequently tell at Eastertime. It is a fictional story built around the incident of the Lord appearing to Simon and his brother on the road to Emmaus. Though it has none of the traditional resurrection story as such, it makes the resurrection very real to almost any age group.

"This is the story of a little orphan girl named Martha, and of the great gift she gave to Jesus. It happened at the time Christ was teaching in Jerusalem, just before He was crucified. Martha lived in the little village of Emmaus near by. She had been left there at the Inn when she was very small, and only dimly remembered the gentle mother who had died. Old Jonas and Sarah had kept her and made her earn her keep with long hours in the kitchen and serving the caravans that stopped at the door".

These *words* are quite different from those of the author, but the facts are accurate. They were gleaned from several *pages* of the original story which I cut from thirty-five minutes reading time to ten.[5]

The Body of the story is just that — it tells the story, the incidents of the plot.

The Conclusion of a story is as important as the conclusion of a lesson or a talk. One should never moralize at the end of a story, yet the listeners must be morally and dramatically satisfied. A story well chosen and well told will point its moral clearly, mentioning it at the end will spoil the punch. The actual climax comes just before the end, but is not usually the ending.

Sometimes the conclusion is a statement which infers a fact. An example is another story I use about the Lord's heal-

---

[5]This story and other story telling material is from a manuscript being prepared by C.B.P. for a book of Stories Prepared for Telling which is not yet ready for publication.

ing of a crippled boy with a hump on his back. The healing is not mentioned, yet the listener is aware when it happens. Then the story ends with these words: "It was not until he (the boy) pulled his shawl more closely about his shoulders that he realized how straight he was standing, how straight he would always stand!"

Another useful conclusion is a quotation which sums up the feeling or impression you wish to leave with the listeners. For example, in a pioneer story of great hardship and struggle and suffering, you may want to sum up all that in the conclusion. In one story in which I took a pioneer woman to her deathbed at the age of ninety-four, I used this for a conclusion: "And when she died at the age of ninety-four, I'm sure the Lord must have sent someone to meet her and say 'Well done, thou good and faithful servant'."

The third way to conclude is the one the Saviour used so often in His parables, which were always lessons in disguise. It is called the epigramatic way, the ending with a question as He did in the story of the Good Samaritan.

When you come to the actual delivery of your story BE ALIVE! Be enthusiastic about the story itself. In fact, never choose a story to tell which you do not like. Live the characters, *feel* their joys and sorrows, their laughter and struggles. Only when you are able to "see" your characters and share their experiences, will you be able to get your listeners to share them too. Spontaneous gestures help make the meaning clear, and the *feeling* you want them to share. So use your body, your eyes, your voice and your expression to help you to paint the picture for your listeners.

The final rule to remember is that when a story is used as part or all of a lesson, then you must tie it in with your objective. Its application to the principle you are teaching should be obvious. Sometimes it would be best to do it before the story, sometimes after the story. One illustration is a story about former President Eisenhower and his faith in prayer. In this one he actually wrought a miracle, and it is an excellent example to use for a lesson on prayer in our personal lives. At the end of the story it could be applied to your lesson with a comment or two, such as, "Without the power of prayer in the lives of this family, the world would have missed a great general . . ." or, to start a discussion, "Was faith in prayer what made this man great"?

The story can be a powerful tool in the hands of a teacher, because it lets us share in great adventures, great moments in history, and great decisions in men's lives. Be willing to give the work and the patience, that you may acquire the knowledge and skill to use this tool wisely. For everyone loves a story, young or old, rich or poor — all can share in rare moments of wonder and delight from a well told story. Best of all is that in that sharing, all may learn the truths we are trying to teach.

POINTS TO REMEMBER

1. There are six major methods of teaching: question and answer; class discussion; lecture; project; role playing; and story telling.

2. There is no magic formula for method selection, but there are several factors to consider: The objective; the time element; and the experience of the group.

3. Student involvement is vital in every method.

4. The two major pitfalls in problem solving are (1) having the solution in your own mind and challenging the class to guess what it is; and (2) asking the type of question which is open to a simple factual answer.

5. Questions have many uses. Good questions should stimulate thought, draw forth comprehensive answers, and be adapted to the experience of the group.

6. Class discussion is very useful if the following rules are kept in mind: Encourage participation; allow freedom of expression; avoid monopoly; keep on the track; see all sides; summarize; reach a decision; and conclude.

7. The lecture method can be useful, but it is the most difficult to make effective, for there is no way to judge whether or not any learning is taking place.

8. The project method is effective because it gives students the opportunity to take the theory of the subject and put it into practice on a problem.

9. Role playing lets students put themselves into the experiences of others, and see how their own behavior affects other people.

10. Story telling is one of the most useful of all methods because it holds attention, teaches attributes of character, and brings understanding more quickly than just words.

11. A good telling story must have action, suspense, a climax, and a minimum of description. Usually it has to be cut and prepared in "telling" words. It also has an introduction, a body, and a conclusion, just as a lesson does.

12. A story can be an introduction to the lesson, the conclusion, or the whole lesson, but it must always lead toward the objective of the lesson.

CHAPTER IX

Tools for Teachers

Audio-Visual aids are to the teacher what a scalpel is to the doctor, a paint brush is to the artist, a chisel to the sculptor: They are necessary as "tools of the trade", but must be used with knowledge and great skill. Every teacher I have known who has used these aids or tools with knowledge and skill, has been an effective teacher.

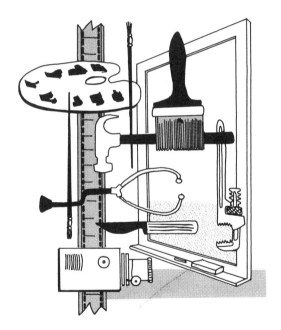

Fig. 69

Tools of the Trade

However, there are two weaknesses inherent in the use of audio-visual aids in teaching. One, some teachers don't use any at all, thus passing up many chances to enhance learning. Two, others misuse them to the point that they become a *substitute* for teaching. The basic purpose for using such tools is to enrich lessons, to be a means to an end rather than the end itself.

Have you ever heard a student say "Why do I forget so much and remember so little?" Many members of the Church who have spent years in Primary and Junior Sunday School, can't even recite the first Article of Faith. Students who have studied the New Testament through two or three classes, admit that they can remember but little of the course contents. Some are not quite sure about the Pharisees and the Sadducees. They know that one group believes in the resurrection, but which one is it?

Some members have studied many phases of Church History but cannot recall the events of the First Vision. Others have spent hours upon hours studying the Book of Mormon. They know that three separate migrations of people are contained in this sacred book, but if you ask them to turn to the record of the Jaredites they cannot do it. Some recall that they once learned that one of the books in the Old Testament is not inspired and is not considered by Latter-day Saints to be scripture. Yet if you ask them to explain which one and why it is so considered, they are at a loss even where to begin.

By thinking through some of the comments below, which were made by college students looking back, perhaps we may find some clues to this problem of forgetting.

Student 1. "I never could see the value of memorizing all the books of the Bible. Some of the books are very important, but others don't seem to have much meaning to us."

Student 2: "I had a course in the New Testament once which stressed the geography of Palestine a great deal. We had to remember in detail the exact size of Galilee, Samaria, and Judea, as well as the general terrain and climate of each. I got through the course all right, and at the time enjoyed it very much. But for the life of me I can't recall a tenth of the facts we covered. At the time I thought that the responsibility of learning so many facts wasn't the best way to teach the New Testament. I thought it was much too mechanical and unrelated to my real interests".

Student 3: "My teacher in Sunday School never seemed able to give very good explanations of gospel truths. He didn't take the time to work out some good examples or illustrations which would enable us to get a clear idea of how religion would help us in our everyday lives. When I got together with my friends outside of class, I found that they too, were confused as to how the class would solve current problems".

In his book "Audio-Visual Methods in Teaching", Edgar Dale gives these three good reasons why we tend to forget what we are taught:

1. We forget when what we are to learn does not seem important to us, either because it lacks importance in itself or because we fail to see any relationship between this new piece of information and things we already know.

2. We forget when we do not make use in our daily living of what we have been asked to learn.

3. We forget when we do not see clearly what it is that we are supposed to be learning. Or when we are not properly shown how to use this new item.[1]

WHY WE USE AUDIO-VISUAL AIDS

If learning is to be permanent, it must be a rich and purposeful experience which is directly related to the interests and needs of the individual. Audio-Visual aids are important in this regard because, by decreasing the abstract element, they help to bring subjects closer to our lives. Specifically audio-visual aids are considered to be important teaching tools because:

1. They speed up learning. Studies conducted during World War II indicated that audio-visual aids cut training time as much as forty percent. The gospel with all its blessings and responsibilities can be taught faster and more effectively by using appropriate audio-visual aids, and using them wisely. Some authorities have said that seventy-five to eighty per cent of what an ordinary person learns is through the eye and the

ear. With so much to learn in so short a time, we cannot neglect the fastest method of learning known.

2. They make learning more permanent. Many studies in education have shown that retention of information is increased fifty to sixty percent when pertinent audio-visual aids are used with other teaching materials. We have often heard the expression "I can remember your face, but I can't recall your name". This is evidence that an impression through sight is more permanent than one received through hearing alone.

3. They make learning more enjoyable. Much has already been said concerning the importance of interest and motivation in learning. To decide whether learning is more enjoyable when audio-visual aids are used, one needs only to sit in on a meeting where they are in use. The old idea that learning must be done the hard mechanical way if it is to be effective, has long been abandoned. Teachers recognize the necessity of making the whole learning and teaching situation pleasant, attractive, and as enjoyable as possible.

4. They compliment and enrich other methods. Story telling is a very interesting method of teaching, and we know Christ was a master at reaching people that way. But few of us *have* the ability to tell stories as He did. Story telling takes on new life when accompanied by suitable visual aids and these aids can often make history a living thing, bringing realism into the classroom.

5. They effect change. The prime purpose of teaching the gospel is to change people's lives for the better. Basic to such changes is the individual's understanding of the factors involved. Because appropriate audio-visual aids make learning faster, more permanent, more accurate, and more enjoyable, the desired life-changes are now more likely to be achieved and be achieved more quickly than would be possible otherwise.

[1]Dale, Edgar, *Audio Visual Methods in Teaching;* p. 12; The Dryden Press, N. Y.

AUDIO-VISUAL AIDS HAVE LIMITATIONS

While audio-visual aids are excellent and necessary tools in assisting teachers to be more effective, they do have their limitations. It has already been pointed out that the most purposeful learning that can occur involves student participation. In other words, students learn more effectively by actually doing things themselves. For instance, if your subject for discussion was service in the Church or for others, you might use recordings of experiences of people who have served; many different kinds of films; pictures; charts; testimonials; and so forth. All of these are wonderful aids in illustrating your objective. However, none of these, nor any combination of these, could begin to be as effective in inspiring the student to serve willingly, as would a well organized individual or class project in actual service, for the ward or the community.

Teachers should keep in mind that any direct or even contrived experience which involves student participation, is far more meaningful in terms of learning, than are those activities which (like audio-visual aids) require only observing or abstract symbolizing. Yet, as Dale points out, life cannot be lived exclusively on either the concrete or the abstract plane of experience. He says further, "We must have both direct and indirect experience. We cannot successfully cope with reality on the indirect, more or less symbolic level, unless we have already had experience on the direct level".[2]

In this connection he suggests that there are three ways of learning something: "(1) We can experience it directly — either through experimenting or through directly and immediately imitating the performance of another person. (2) We can observe the performance of another person but postpone doing it ourselves. (3) We can learn, by reading or listening, about experiences that others have had. Each step is successively further removed from the actual doing".[3] We can conclude that direct student involvement gives us a foundation, a sound basis for indirect experiencing. "But all experience, no matter how concrete or how abstract, and no

[2]*Ibid,* page 73. [3]*Ibid,* page 73. [4]*Ibid,* page 74.

matter what the instructional medium, must finally be tied firmly together if they are to be means and ends in an organic process of learning."[4]

To sum up, as effective and necessary as audio-visual aids are, they do not take the place of direct experience; and as important as direct experiences are, we also need audio-visual aids. Therefore, the two mediums must work together.

THREE TYPES OF AUDIO-VISUAL AIDS

In general, there are three types of audio-visual aids used in teaching: Those that illustrate; mechanical presentation; and objects. It is not the purpose of this Chapter to discuss in detail the philosophy or use of these aids, but to point out their place in the learning process. There are many excellent books and pamphlets currently in print which will give the teacher valuable assistance in developing a realistic approach to the use of these aids. For example, Woodruff's manual "Teaching the Gospel" has three chapters which contain a good deal of such information and help.

A-V AIDS THAT ILLUSTRATE

While most all audio-visual aids are illustrative in nature, the term as used here refers to such things as chalkboards, flannel boards, groove boards, peg boards, sand boxes, charts, graphs, pictures, et cetera. The chalkboard is by far the most practical aid since it is the most accessible and has multiple uses. In his article "Make Your Blackboard a Vital Aid", William E. Berrett tells us that with the blackboard as a visual aid, five important phases of the teaching process can be utilized. They are:

1. Getting attention.
2. Motivating thought and study.
3. Clarifying the subject or object under discussion.
4. Obtaining student retention of ideas.
5. Obtaining student activity.[5]

Even more than the chalkboard does, pictures, flannel boards and groove boards often give us a clearer mental picture of the subject or place being discussed. Some give a third

---

[5]Reiser, A. Hamer; *A Reader for the Teacher:* Deseret Book Co., 1960.

Fig. 70

Graphs, Charts, etc.

dimensional quality, such as the peg board and the groove board, which makes these "pictures" even more realistic. Charts and graphs tend to compare progress or break down statistics to a visually understandable form. Maps are useful in giving us images of distances and locations. And all these aids help to satisfy the feeling that "If I see it, I can remember it".

MECHANICAL PRESENTATIONS

By "mechanical presentations" we mean those that require some mechanical equipment to use. This would include motion pictures, film strips, tapes, slides, and so forth. Although these presentations are illustrative too, they differ from the chalk-board-flannel board type of aid in several ways.

One is that they usually take a longer period of time to present, as compared with the time it takes to show a picture, for instance. Another is, they usually cover a variety of thoughts, whereas most purely illustrative aids tend to deal with a single idea or concept. A third difference is in the need

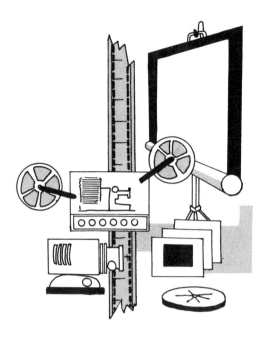

Fig. 71

Mechanical

for advance preparation of students before using a mechanical aid. This is because they are not only exceptional for illustrating points, but are also excellent investigative and thought provoking devices. Some exceptions to this would be, certain slide presentations used to picture one particular subject; short recordings inspiring thoughts; poems, readings; and recordings used to furnish backgrounds or mood-setting music. We can see that these preparations would seldom be needed with most illustrative aids. A further point to remember about using mechanical presentations is that they should never be used merely as entertainment, unless *entertainment* is your objective.

One of the greatest values of mechanical presentations is their ability to "give us experiences". Since we are all limited in the amount of first-hand experience we can have in a fast expanding world, it is vital to our learning that we utilize other means of "experiencing". It is through these other means (motion pictures and so forth) that we can tour Bible lands, return to the Carthage jail to witness a martyrdom, or make a journey with Moses into the wilderness.

UTILIZING MECHANICAL PRESENTATIONS

When a mechanical audio-visual aid has been selected for use by the teacher, there are five areas he should consider if the experience is to be meaningful. First, the teacher should have prepared himself, by having clearly established goals and a real purpose for using the aid. After selecting the best presentation for the job at hand, he should preview the film or aid and coordinate it with the lesson. Second, prepare the students. Since the aid may be used as an introduction to a lesson, as the direct teaching of the lesson, or as a lesson review, it is important to tell them what to look for as they watch. This can be done by outlining the important things to observe, either on the chalkboard or in student handouts. Third, prepare the physical facilities for the best use of the particular aid. Power equipment should be set up in advance, with proper power supply to operate it. Also, check to be sure it is working properly. Room ventilation and temperature control should be checked along with the desired seating arrangement.

Fourth, follow up the presentation with student participation which will give impetus to study. Such activities as class discussion, question-answer, panels, research projects, and course reviews are all excellent methods to use in such follow ups. Fifth, evaluate the material presented. After every presentation the teacher should determine whether or not the lesson objectives were achieved. This can be done by evaluating the student participation that followed the presentation.

OBJECTS AS TEACHING AIDS

An object lesson is one in which a teacher uses visible, tangible, familiar objects (a magnet, berry boxes, articles of food, etc.) to make an analogy to a point of doctrine or an idea. For example, a teacher might come to class wearing a long feathery carrot top in his lapel or a pocket, creating both interest and curiosity. During the course of his lesson he would point out that this carrot worn on the outside of his body, does his body no more good than does our religion if it is not learned and utilized.

Fig. 72

Objects

Another time the teacher might bring three berry boxes to class: One could be filled with fruit or candy, one filled with rusty nails, and one left empty. The following points could then be made: The berry boxes are all nearly alike, and they are worth just whatever is put into them. Now compare these boxes with our lives. The boxes of our lives — our bodies — are nearly all alike. They are containers like the berry boxes, and we are constantly filling them with things. We fill them with good things, like prayer, faith, service, wholesome reading, and so forth; or with bad things like wasted time, trashy movies and books, and gossiping; or we leave them empty. Like the boxes, our lives are worth exactly what we put into them. If they are as empty as some of the berry boxes, they are cheap, worth little to either ourselves or the world. But gospel-filled lives are worth more than man can pay. These two examples suggest three uses for object lessons: One as purely illustrative, used as a springboard into a lesson; another as the greater part of a lesson or the framework around which you build a lesson; and a third, as a clincher to a lesson. Any object, the use of which is well understood by the class, can be employed to compare reality with abstract, hard-to-visualize concepts.

To sum up the fascinating and worthwhile field of audio-visual aids as tools for teachers, it must be pointed out that though they are very often necessary and enjoyable for teachers to use, they are only effective in making learning more permanent if they are varied, and if they accomplish the objective better than it could be done by the teacher.

POINTS TO REMEMBER:

1. Audio-visual aids are the "tools of the trade" for the teacher; but they must be used with knowledge and skill.
2. They must not be allowed to become a substitute for teaching.
3. Audio-visual aids are useful because they help to bring abstract subjects closer to our lives.
4. Audio-visual aids speed up learning, make it more permanent and enjoyable. They enrich other methods and help effect changes in the lives of students.
5. The great limitation of Audio-visual aids is that none of them can be as effective as first-hand experience. None-the-less, we need indirect experience as well.
6. There are three general types of audio-visual aids: illustrative, mechanical, and objects.
7. The chalkboard is considered by many to be the most practical aid because of its accessibility and multiple uses.
8. Mechanical presentations (such as motion pictures) take more time, but usually cover many concepts.
9. Students must be prepared by the teacher before mechanical presentations can be really effective.
10. Almost any familiar object can be used to make an analogy to a point of doctrine or an idea.
11. Audio-visual aids are effective only when they are varied, and if they accomplish the objective better than the teacher could do it.

CHAPTER X

If You Want Smooth Sailing

"Bill Smith, this is the third time I've asked you to keep quiet! Now one more sound out of you and I'm going to send you to the Bishop's office". This experience is not uncommon. It is repeated week after week in Church classes everywhere. Francis Parker once said, "The fundamental reason why children do not act right is because they do not have the conditions for right action". The presence of disciplinary problems in a classroom is symptomatic of fundamental deficiencies in the teaching situation. In other words, good classes do not just happen.

We have already considered some of the ingredients a teacher must include in his own life, and in the classroom, if he is to be a success. Now let us pursue the subject a little further. Above all, teachers need to be realistic. If we have taken the time to know and understand each person in our group, we may find things in their lives that cannot be changed immediately or even over a long period. Some of the situations we uncover may be the very cause of an individual behaving in the manner he does. For example, what can you do if (1) Bill's parents are about to be divorced; or (2) his mother is incurably ill; or (3) his father's income is not sufficient to properly support the family? Yet, any or all of these conditions can contribute to the attitude and behavior that Bill brings to class. This still does not give Bill the license to disrupt the learning process of the entire group. For while we want to follow the example and admonition of the Savior in leaving the ninety and nine in order to seek the one, the Lord certainly did not imply that we should lose the ninety-nine while attempting to reach that one. If Bill's behavior is negative, he must come to realize that in Church, as in any social situation, he is expected to act and perform according to the accepted standard.

SET A STANDARD

Fig. 73

Set a Standard

In Church classes, as in life, ground rules need to be established to govern human behavior. Students need to know and understand the role they are expected to play and what they must do to make learning meaningful. It is best if the students themselves can set up class rules and regulations under the direction of the teacher. It is important that they be given a voice in setting up these regulations, since they are less likely to resist their own decisions. However, there may be times when the teacher has to set up the rules himself. Most educators believe that students gain in security and poise when they know what is "off limits" and what is within bounds.

Teachers are doing their students and the Church a great disservice if they do not set good classroom standards and hold to them, since neither learning nor the Spirit of the Lord can be present in an environment that is characterized by rowdiness, lack of courtesy and general indifference. Teachers then, have the responsibility of seeing that such conditions do not exist, and it is their duty to see that the "Bills" do conform to the accepted and "agreed upon" program.

While the conditions described here are typical of the elementary and secondary age groups, it is not meant to suggest that discipline problems do not exist with adults. Older students may not speak out of turn, throw objects, tilt chairs or jab a neighbor in the ribs, but they will show their general disinterest by looking through a wallet, cleaning out a purse, whispering to a neighbor, or just day dreaming. Though standards themselves do not solve all problems, they are vital to good teaching. Studies have shown that students of all ages learn best when they know what is expected of them.

INTEREST IS THE KEY

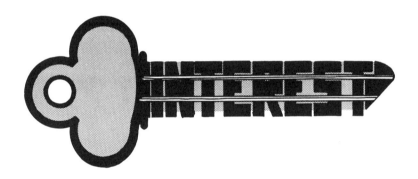

Fig. 74

Interest is the Key

Before discussing how to set up class standards, it is necessary to consider another equally important principle of maintaining good discipline, that of creating interest. Motivation and interest and their relationship to student needs have already been discussed. But their importance to learning and good classroom control cannot be emphasized too strongly; for where there is genuine interest in the subject, and motivation of students, there is never any need for discipline. An interested student who is actively involved in the subject is rarely a problem.

UTILIZING STUDENT'S TALENTS

One of the first steps in setting up class standards is to get the members to help decide the regulations by which they will be governed. Remember, people will tend to support those things in which they have a part. Take the time to ask them what they **want** out of the class. List the answers on the chalkboard so all can study them. Then say something like "OK, how are WE going to accomplish this? What will we do when and if some member of the class doesn't follow the rules we set up?" Again write the answers on the board and when they have agreed, have the class secretary write them down for future reference or have them duplicated so that each class member will have his own personal copy.

While class democracy is vital in establishing rules, the teacher should always retain the right to change or amend student decisions. It should be clearly understood that if learning is not accomplished under the students' rules, then the rules must be changed. Also, tactfully point out that while you are happy to let them make as many of the rules and decisions as possible, there are some basic things which they cannot change. For instance, the students cannot be permitted to change the class meeting place or time, if it is a regularly scheduled part of an auxiliary. Nor could they change the basic subject being studied. But they could help decide the approach to a particular part of the subject, or a project. They could help decide what steps would be taken with one who breaks the "ground rules" laid down by the class.

Class officers can be appointed or elected to assist the teacher in the planning and operation of each class. Generally speaking, class leaders can be used in all age groups from the primary grade to the senior adult class. Utilizing student participants is an excellent way to help build and develop the "we" concept and group morale, as discussed in Chapter

Fig. 75

*Student Officers can Assist the Teacher in the
Planning and Operation of each Class*

III. In addition to the class spirit that can be developed,
appointing officers presents the teacher with an ideal opportunity to train lay members for positions of leadership. It is
suggested that teachers appoint their class leaders rather than
elect them; for too often elections become popularity contests,
with the winners having little of either ability or inclination
to accomplish the tasks of leadership.

Frequently the position of class president or vice-president
means little to class members because these offices have come
to mean nothing more than titles. Positions of leadership need
to carry with them both responsibility and dignity. This can
be achieved by developing a program of leadership training
within the group itself. Each class is an embryonic ward. Instead of electing class officers, have the class list with you on
the board, the qualities of leadership they desire in a leader.
After the teacher has considered these listed desires of the
group, and the individual abilities within the group, then

with an attitude of prayer he can properly call class officers to serve. This approach provides many good opportunities for students to learn why the Church selects and sustains leaders in the manner it does.

Private personal interviews should also be a part of the teacher's approach in selecting an individual to serve. If the class members are young students who are living with parents or guardians, then these people should be interviewed too. Much dignity and pride in the office can be achieved by using this method. The interviews give teachers a chance to raise such questions as "Can and will you serve your class in this responsible position? Will you devote the required time to this assignment?" And to the parents, "Will you support your son or daughter in this calling? Do you fully understand his need to be in class every week and on time? And the need to spend some out-of-class time working on this assignment?"

If class officers are given this kind of understanding and support, it is relatively easy to enlist their energies in giving direction to other members. And their work will help the teacher do a better job. You will find that the class with active officers is usually the class with the fewest problems. By developing good student rapport and support, teachers can use class members and leaders in the planning and operation of the class. When student leaders have a share in the responsibility of operating the class, it soon becomes "our" class, not Brother "Blank's" class. It is amazing how classes respond to the direction and guidance given by members of their own group.

GOOD LEADERSHIP NEEDS TO BE DEVELOPED

Like successful classes, good leadership doesn't just happen. Class officers need to have the opportunity to learn the mechanics of leadership, and the chance to develop and perfect these skills in a Church environment. Therefore, teachers should provide every possible opportunity for students to gain practical experience. Our present and future leaders can

Fig. 76

Good Leadership Needs to be Developed

learn much by personally participating in such activities as the following:

1. Planning a meeting.
2. Constructing an agenda.
3. Leading a discussion.
4. Conducting a meeting.
5. Preparing and presenting a talk.
6. Making an assignment.
7. Planning a class project.
8. Evaluating a lesson presentation.
9. Making an announcement.

MAINTAINING GOOD CLASSROOM CONTROL

Establishing class standards, creating interest in subject matter, and utilizing student abilities are all important in maintaining good classroom control. Yet lay teachers are always anxious to have concrete suggestions on how to prevent common classroom problems. Therefore, let us now consider some of the things good teachers have found to be successful in this regard.

Fig. 77

Learn to "ride your eye" over the class

1. Learn to "ride your eye" over the entire class. It is of considerable advantage to the teacher to stand where he can see clearly what every person is doing. (See suggested seating arrangements illustrated in Chapter III). Move around. Try to hear and see all that is happening in the class all of the time. Let them know that you can see each of them.

2. Learn the names of your class members as soon as possible. It would be helpful to have an assignment, or a variety of things to do the first day that would enable students to get acquainted with each other and the teacher. Completing information on personal inventory forms would be one suggestion. A teacher should be able to call any class member by name within the first two weeks. Getting to know students is the best way to gain their confidence and support.

3. Learn, by practice, to bring into the discussion those students whose attention is wavering. It is far easier to

Fig. 78

Learn the Names of your Class members early

reach them before they get interested in something other than the subject, than to try to bring them back once they have made the break. If they do get interested in other things, it may be a sign to the teacher that his method of teaching, or the material being taught, is not meeting the students' needs.

4. Be businesslike. Keep an adult reserve of formality which students know is there. Don't try to "be one of them". Keep students busy with a variety of activities. Begin promptly, and with a suggestion of vigor. Close your period on time. Utilize student abilities, holding every member of the class responsible for all that takes place during the period. Remember that a class without standards is like a car without a steering wheel.

5. Make every effort to avoid all suggestion of criticism, disorganization, or anger before the class. Maintain a poise that is characteristic of efficiency and success. Be genuine, humble, and *use a sense of humor*. Frequently, delicate

situations arise from personality conflicts; situations which could be potential discipline problems if not handled properly. For instance, a student might give a "smart" answer to a teacher, expecting to upset him and get called down. This is a problem which sometimes occurs during the time that a new teacher is being accepted by a class. Instead of reprimanding the student, the teacher can often turn the comment into a humorous situation, either laughing at himself or showing the class a different side to the comment. Either one will usually ease the tension that might have existed.

6. Remain calm, dignified, but firm, when confronted with a behavior problem. While this is much easier to suggest than to do, never-the-less it is fundamental to the ultimate welfare of both the student and the teacher. If the class, under the direction of the teacher, has developed a set of standards before the offense occurs, then the teacher can better decide the course of action which will be fair and consistent with the expectations of the group. Most serious offenses should be dealt with in private. Above all, the welfare of the person involved must be our basic consideration. If a person (elementary or secondary age) is interfering with the work or learning of the others and you are not certain what to do, do nothing *then*. After class go to him in private, discuss the matter, and request his cooperation. Many times class officers can be of real assistance in reaching the more difficult students. For instance, young people are more worried about the impression they are making on their peer group (other students) than on the teacher. Therefore, if their duties are structured to carry the proper authority, class officers can often squelch behavior problems quicker, with less animosity and more effectiveness than can the teacher. Do nothing yourself that you can get your students to do for you, even though they do it less efficiently — the problem is for them to work out if possible, and they like to help. They like nothing better than to be asked, "What shall WE do about this?" Students should not be sent

from the room except for serious forms of misbehavior, such as open defiance even after all other forms of discipline have been tried and failed; or as you follow the rules which have been set up with the group and the local administrators of your organization.

7. Use special occasions to let students know you are interested in them. Many teachers do not realize the numerous opportunities they have to win the confidence of class members. A nice letter, telephone call, or a visit to the home when a person is ill, will work wonders in enlisting the student's future support.

8. Stop the little things before they become major problems. Quite often when students feel that they can "get away with it", they will test the teacher to see just how far he will let them go before calling a halt.

9. Keep a tight rein. It is far easier for a teacher to relax some control, than to try to develop stronger control after he has encountered a problem. It would be well for a teacher to begin his assignment by showing students his

Fig. 79   *Keep a Tight Rein*

firm side; then gradually easing up on the reins as students come to realize the potential within him. Being a "good Joe" is not the answer. Students need to know from the beginning that the teacher will stand firm when he is right.

10. Be self-confident. Have courage, moral courage to face the situation. It is hard to appear self-confident, but it is a first essential. These three things will help: (A) be well prepared; (B) use a lot of variety, and enlist the help of class members as much as possible, to put over the lessons; and (C) be prayerful. There is no substitute for prayer.

11. Be enthusiastic about your subject and it will kindle a similar response in your group. Remember, as one teacher was heard to say, "The problem that looms like a mountain of disaster at the end of a tired day often decreases to molehill significance after a refreshing period of rest. The Lord surely had classroom teachers in mind when He put a night between two days".

12. *Don't confuse discipline with punishment.* The purpose of discipline is to help students grow toward new insights and understanding. The purpose of punishment is to restore discipline. Punishment is quick action on the part of the teacher; discipline is a long term series of actions involving both student and teacher. Punishment brings to account past actions. Discipline looks forward to the improvement of future actions. Punishment centers on the individual and should never be administered to an entire group. Good discipline depends on the harmonious relationship among members of the group. Whether or not this is achieved, depends in large measure on the teacher.

POINTS TO REMEMBER:

1. The presence of disciplinary problems is symptomatic of fundamental deficiencies in the teaching situation.

2. In the beginning, and with their help, set up behavior standards or ground rules for the class.

3. Discipline is a problem in adult classes too. Adult misbehavior merely takes a different form.

4. Interest is the key: the interested student, actively involved in the subject is rarely a problem.
5. Utilize student talents. Get them to help decide and do as much as possible in the classroom, but reserve the right to change or amend any rule that does not work.
6. Class officers should be appointed by the teacher after prayerful consideration; private interviews with both student and his parents; as well as decisions by class members on what qualities they want in their leaders.
7. Good leadership has to be *developed*. Our class activities can train the future leaders of the Church if students are given practical experience.
8. Some specific suggestions for coping with classroom problems are:

   A. Learn to "ride your eye" over the entire class.

   B. Learn names of class members as soon as possible.

   C. Practice bringing into discussion the student whose attention is wavering — it's easier than doing it later.

   D. Be businesslike, keep an adult reserve of formality they *know* is there; don't try to be "one of the kids".

   E. Maintain a poise characteristic of efficiency and success, be humble, and use a sense of humor.

   F. Remain calm, dignified, and firm, no matter how difficult it is.

   G. The welfare of the student is our basic consideration.

   H. Show the students that you are interested in them.

   I. Start with a tight rein and relax after the firmness has been established.

   J. Have the moral courage to face the situation, and always be prayerful.

   K. Be enthusiastic about your subject.

9. Don't confuse punishment with discipline.

10. Good discipline is long range and depends on the harmonious relationship among members of the group. It is largely the responsibility of the teacher to bring about this relationship.

CHAPTER XI

Have You Opened Their Eyes?

"He who governs well leads the blind; he who teaches them gives them eyes".[1] How will you know if your teaching is opening the eyes of your students unless you make periodic checks on their progress? In secular schools, checks are made in order to give a grade (a rating of performance and accomplishment) by evaluating the progress of the students. No grade as such is given to either teacher or student in the Church class. But the Church teacher does need to check periodically to determine whether or not his teaching is effectively helping the students to retain facts and modify behavior. For this purpose he needs to give tests, evaluate the results and keep records of individual progress. In the process he needs to teach students to look at themselves objectively, set their own goals or objectives, and to evaluate their own performances. He will find this easier to do if he applies it first to himself and his own performance.

EVALUATION AND THE LEARNING PROCESS

Before we came to understand that evaluation was an integral part of learning, most teaching was organized around the *assign-study-recite-test formula*. This tended to make grades or competitive marks the goal instead of the ability to apply principles. That traditional formula demonstrates entirely different thinking from today's Five Steps of Learning: *exposure, repetition, understanding, conviction, application*, as discussed in Chapter VI.

One of the ultimate goals of education is to develop in the student the ability to set up his own goals and guide his own learning, both of which are a continuing process throughout life. This involves self-direction and self-motivation, which at best are a result of self-appraisal. But if the evaluation is im-

---

[1]McKay, David O., *Gospel Ideals for Living*, p. 139.

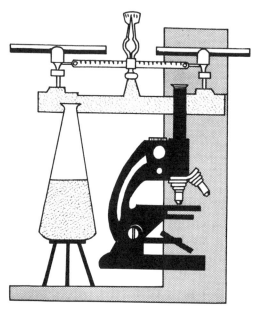

Fig. 80

"Evaluation is an Integral Part of Learning"

posed upon the student without his acceptance of the goals as important, the results will have little meaning or value to him.

Testing, as we wish to discuss it, is a very positive process. It is not done to determine how little a student knows, but to help him evaluate his growth in the subject area. Therefore, let us use tests in our Church classes to teach him how to set up a goal and reach it, then to evaluate his own performance. The greater part he has in choosing and setting up the problem, as well as finding a solution, the more receptive he will be to the answer and to the appraising of his performance by you and by himself. Even more important, the greater will be his learning.

EVALUATION VERSUS MEASUREMENT

Most tests that we give students, "measure" their factual knowledge or skills. Other types such as essay-question tests, problem-solving tests, and some true-false tests are attempts to "evaluate" students' ability to think for themselves, the ability to express themselves, and the ability to apply principles learned. Therefore, we need to have our goals in mind as we prepare tests. As Chuch teachers we are mostly concerned with building behavior patterns which will lead our people to eternal life. While living the principles of the gospel will make this life easier and happier, our main goal is building for eternity. This means that we are concerned always with the total behavior of the student, and that is what we seek to evaluate. Facts are necessary, so we need to use tests that measure retention of facts. But tests using problem-solving will show whether the student has learned how to apply facts and principles to life; they will show changes in attitudes, interests, ideals, and understanding. Thus, they are more useful in evaluating the whole student, and we should use them as often as possible.

BASIC STEPS IN EVALUATION

Whether you are using a simple true-false test or attempting to evaluate changes in behavior and attitudes, certain fundamental procedures need to be used. Learn them for they will be constantly helpful to you as you attempt to evaluate the growth of your students.

I. **State your objectives clearly.** Only then will you be able to identify the changes you are seeking to achieve. For instance, if you were teaching an Old Testament class for teenagers in Sunday School, you might list some of the objectives as follows:

A. To teach them facts concerning the:
1. Number of books and their names.
2. Chronology of major events.
3. Names of Prophets.

B. To teach them how to use the Bible and how to read scripture aloud.

C. To bring them to an understanding of the Ten Commandments and their significance today.

D. To help them to understand the prophecies which were fulfilled in the Christ, and in the restoration of the Church in latter days.

II. **Define each of the general objectives in terms of student behavior.** For example, No. C might be defined thus:

C. To bring them to an understanding of the Ten Commandments and their significance today:

1. Does the student know their origin, why they were given?
2. Does he understand all the words used?
3. Does he recognize their validity in today's society?
4. Does he understand that if practiced today they will lead him to the living of the higher law as voiced by the Savior?
5. Does he apply them to his own life?

III. **Devise problem-solving situations in which students may reveal the desired behavior or thinking you are seeking to develop.** For instance, on the commandment to keep the Sabbath Day holy, give them an actual situation to work out:

To illustrate: An LDS man who works six days a week finds that Sunday is the only time he has to do his yard work. He is an active member of the Church and realizes he is expeced to set a good example in *all* that he does. This does include a well kept yard, but he cannot afford a gardner. Keeping in mind the observance of the Sabbath, how can this man solve his problem realistically?

Here's another: A young LDS couple want to get married. They are very much in love, but he still has two years of college before he can graduate and become an effective provider. The decision as to whether they should wait until his education is completed or marry now, is a difficult one for them to make. They are aware that many students in similar situations drop out of school after marriage. It becomes clear to them that they must seek counsel. If they came to you, how would you advise them?

IV. **Keep a record of student behavior in order to evaluate his progress.** Do not leave this to your memory or you may be influenced by the intensity of the most recent situation, or fail to take into account the differences in the various situations and the reaction to them. If you ask a student to do a special assignment, jot down (on his permanent record card in your confidential file) his attitude, how well or how poorly he filled the requirement, and any other pertinent observations and information.

V. The final step in this evaluation process is to **interpret the recorded behavior in the light of your objectives.** The record itself is NOT the evaluation, the record reveals only WHAT was done. You should appraise this against what was desired, and in the light of *all* you know of the student and the situation. Then you will be able to see how far and how fast he is progressing. The important thing to remember in evaluating is that we are constantly seeking to improve student understanding of gospel areas and how they relate to individual lives.

CONSTRUCTING TESTS

There are many types of tests available commercially. However, the average teacher gives many more tests of his own devising than tests prepared by others. This is especially true of the Church teacher. This means it is important that we understand some of the basic rules about tests and their construction, so that we can construct for ourselves a few simple tests which we will find of great value in checking the progress of our classes.

A. Define the objectives.

B. Provide situations whereby the objectives can be reached by the students.

C. Measure the results obtained, to see to what extent the objectives have been reached.

If the objectives have been reached, then the teacher can be assured that they are attainable, and that his procedures for gathering and arranging materials have been satisfactory. On the other hand, if many of the students have failed to reach the objectives, then both objectives and procedures need to be reviewed and modified. Without this final process of testing and evaluating the results, futile objectives and inadequate experiences will continue, and will tend to become hardened into habit and custom. Many ineffective teachers have been teaching for years without evaluation or modification of their methods and procedures. They may have had a high potential in the beginning, but their ineffective practices have long since settled into custom. Because they "get by" week after week, they feel that time alone makes them good teachers. Occasionally we need to remind ourselves that practice makes perfect only when we are practicing the right thing.

The objective you have agreed upon will determine the type of test to be constructed. In general, objectives fall into four categories: (1) facts, information, and skills; (2) techniques and methods; (3) types of mental processes such as the capacity to interpret data and to collect and organize it; (4) attitudes, ideals, interests, and values.

Once the objectives have been defined, they must then be analyzed to determine what can be achieved in a specific length of time. At this point, the *teacher must decide which type of test will most clearly indicate the achievement of each objective.* With these thoughts in mind, let us look at the different types of tests which any of us can construct:

I. **The Essay-type Question test.** Theoretically, this is the ideal, for it requires a student to think, to sift his thoughts and to apply them intelligently to the questions at hand. But like many theories, in practice the essay-type question has many weaknesses. Essay questions, introduced by words like discuss, describe, explain, or compare, are meant to develop the thinking of the student. But many times this thinking is not evaluated with fairness and consistency. This weakness was graphically illustrated by one study made in England wherein seven evaluators graded the same forty-eight papers. Evaluator A failed only one student; B didn't fail any; C failed seven; D failed none; E failed five; F failed two; and G failed nineteen!

There are other weaknesses as well, such as answers given in generalities gleaned from reading or conversation instead of from thinking; or misinterpreting of a question so that the student gives a well thought out answer but from the wrong direction. How should he be evaluated? Further, some have good facts but no logic in their presentation, which again defeats the purpose because it shows a lack of clear thinking. Finally, the necessary narrowness of the sample being tested is a definite weakness of this method of testing. This latter means that because of the length of time it takes to do an essay-type answer, a student can be judged only on a small portion of the course material.

None-the-less, a wisely chosen essay-type question is good practice for the student in thinking through a problem, and gives valuable information on his progress to the teacher. Here are some samples:

ESSAY-TYPE QUESTIONS:

A. **Discuss** each of the nine points in Joseph Smith's platform, noting the number which have been put into effect today.

B. **Describe** the building and planting projects at Garden Grove, Mt. Pisgah, Council Bluffs, and Winter Quarters. **Evaluate** the merits of Brigham Young's "filling station" plan for the westward movement.

C. **Describe** and **discuss** the function and purpose of the Kirtland temple and compare with the construction of modern temples.

D. **Compare** the Protestant statement on the personality of God as found in the Nicean Creed with the statement found in the Doctrine and Covenants 130:22.

E. **Explain** what is meant by the statement "The Fatherhood of God and the brotherhood of man".

II. SHORT ANSWER TESTS BASED ON RECALL
There are two types of tests based on recall; (1) Simple recall, and (2) Sentence completion tests. Let us examine both.

A. **Simple Recall** is one of the oldest methods of attempting to objectify student responses to tests. In other words, make answers objective or real, rather than the thinking-opinions of the students. For this reason, simple recall tests are used most when the objective is to check the student's knowledge of facts, information, or skills. This procedure differs from the essay-type question by limiting the answer to one word or one brief phrase. You will find that most complicated questions, the type that could be used for essay answers, can be broken down into several questions requiring very brief answers. This is especially true if you want factual or objective answers rather than thinking-opinion answers. However, care must be taken to phrase the questions in such a way that the answers are definite and short, preferably one word. This means that the material on which the test is based must be definite and factual rather than philosophical.

The answer blanks should be long enough for legible answers to be written, and should be placed in a vertical column to the right of the questions. Further, it is most important that all acceptable answers should be listed on your scoring sheet so that your scoring can be objective as well.

Simple Recall Questions:

1. In what year was the Prophet Joseph Smith born?   ....
2. Where was the first temple built after the restoration of the Church? ....
3. What year was the Restored Church organized?   ....
4. How many temples are in use today?   ....
5. Who betrayed the Christ to the Romans?   ....

B. **Sentence Completion Tests** are simple sentences from which one or more words have been deleted so that the student can fill them in. The sentences should be definite and clearly stated. If you are testing for understanding, then re-word the entire sentence. If you are testing for rote memory, then copy the sentence directly from the text. Blanks may occur at any place in the sentence, though if a blank comes at the end of the sentence, it becomes a matter of simple recall. Blanks should possess these three characteristics in common: (1) they should all be the same length; (2) all should be numbered; and (3) the correspondingly numbered blanks should be placed in a vertical column to the right or left of the sentences. In general, the blanks should require but one word; and the larger the number of blanks the more difficult the test.

The sentence completion test is used most effectively in checking the understanding of a complex idea from a whole paragraph. Used in this manner, it requires the same kind of higher thought processes as the ideal essay-type question.

Advantages and **Disadvantages** in recall type tests:

The **advantages:** Since these questions require recall rather than recognition, guessing is reduced to a minimum. One can be assured that the path followed in the solution of the problem is largely controlled. As compared with the usual essay-type, it directs the thought process toward a definite goal and prevents padding and bluffing. Further, it is a form frequently used and will be familiar to most students; it is economical of space, easy to construct, and allows a wide sampling of the subject material in a comparatively short time.

The **disadvantages:** These types are hard to score unless they are being used to test just for knowledge of facts; in which case it becomes a matter of measuring rote memory only. Probably this is their greatest disadvantage, for it is difficult to make up questions for simple recall and sentences completion tests which call for real thinking.

III. SHORT ANSWER TESTS BASED ON RECOGNI-
TION

Three types of short-answer test will be described. These
tests are based on the capacity of the individual to recognize the correct answer from among several presented.
They are (A) multiple-choice test, (B) true-false tests,
and (C) matching word or phrase tests.

A. **Multiple-Choice:** In the type of short answer test
known as **multiple-choice,** the right answer to a question appears among a number (usually three or four)
of wrong ones. *Unless these wrong ones are as plausible as the correct one, the purpose of the test will
be defeated*: because the answers that are not plausible are eliminated immediately and the student
can then make his choice almost by elimination.
These plausbile wrong answers are called "distractors". If the student is careless in his thinking or
is ignorant on the subject, the distractors may lead
him to the wrong answer. Distractors that have a
logical or bookish connotation will be more effective,
forcing more thought to choose the correct answer.
Another factor which will add to the plausibility of
the alternate answers is their homogeneity or uni-
formity. The more alike all the answers are, the
more discrimination is required in choosing the correct one. An excellent example can be found in the
"Word Power" section of the Reader's Digest, in
which it often takes considerable skill to decide
which choice comes closest to the exact meaning of
the word. Here are other examples which are built
around Church teachings:

Multiple Choice Examples:

1. The Church now sponsors mostly what kind of
   education?
   (a) Secular education
   (b) Professional education
   (c) Education for the trades
   (d) General education
   (e) Religious education

2. Check the *three* features of the Mormon society which aroused most opposition in the early days of the Church.
   (a) The solidarity and exclusiveness of the Saints.
   (b) Their attitude toward the American Indian.
   (c) Difference in religious beliefs.
   (d) Proselyting activities.
   (e) Their New England origin.
   (f) Their type of city planning.

3. The Word of Wisdom teaches which *two* of the following:
   (a) Meat is better than grain or fruit in warm weather.
   (b) Fruits and vegetables are best when dried or preserved.
   (c) Temperance should be exercised in all things.
   (d) We should avoid all artificially flavored beverages.
   (e) Meat should be used sparingly.

4. To be humble means to be:
   (a) Cowardly
   (b) Teachable
   (c) Easily humiliated
   (d) Lacking in determination
   (e) Reserved

5. One of the following is not the function of a Prophet:
   (a) To tell when the Savior will return to this earth.
   (b) To cry repentance to the people.
   (c) To speak forth for God.
   (d) To interpret God's will to man.
   (e) To hold the keys or directing power of the Priesthood.

Advantages and disadvantages of the multiple-choice test:

The multiple-choice form is the most flexible of all the forms of short-answer tests. Its alternate answers may be so near together in meaning that it will take much keenness of discrimination to distinguish among them. Or they may be used simply to test for information acquired by rote. They are better than the simple-recall form in complicated or ambiguous problems. The realiability of this form is high.

The **disadvantages** are several: They are difficult to construct. It takes as much time to construct one good multiple-choice item as to construct three or four simple-recall or true-false items. And it occupies as much space on the page. Also, plausible alternatives are often hard to find, and this form takes more of the class time to answer.

IV. **TRUE OR FALSE TESTS:** In this form of short answer test, the student is asked to render a judgment about the statement as a whole. Usually the judgment rendered is whether the statement is true or false, hence its name. It can be used in almost any field of learning to evaluate the materials as well as the mental processes involved. The statement should not be lifted bodily from a textbook with some slight change in the wording to make them false. It is much better to have the idea imbedded in a fresh array of words. The language should be within the comprehension of those taking the test. That is, do not use long or difficult words which many might not understand. The statement should be clear and unambiguous (not open to misinterpretation); and its meaning should not be clouded by double negatives and too many qualifying clauses. Whenever possible, specific descriptive statements are better than ambiguous indicators of comparison like "more" and "less".

Also, certain "determiners" of the truth of falsity of a statement should be avoided. Sentences using such determiners as "totally", "entirely", "completely", "solely", "absolutely", "always", "never", "only", "alone", are usually false. While sentences using "should", "may", "most", "some", and "often", are more than apt to be true. (This is a thing quickly learned by young people and may make your findings unreliable). By actual count of words, it has been shown that long sentences, with more than twenty words, are likely to be true.

An effective modification of the true-false test would be to instruct the student to correct with one word each false question, but to do nothing to the true statements. Not only to say a statement is wrong, but to have to correct it requires knowledge and thinking. This further eliminates chance and guesswork.

Advantages and disadvantages of the true-false test:

When properly constructed, this short-answer form can be made to sample a large number of items in a short time. It is comparatively easy to construct and score, although its scoring is not as indicative of the students' ability as other forms because of the possibility of guessing. Many questions can be put on one page, making it economical of space as well as of classroom time.

Its **disadvantages** stem mostly from carelessly constructed tests, since it is so easy to insert one of the qualifying words listed above which will give clues to the student. If the student learns to look for such clues, he will do little thinking and you may find yourself evaluating his cleverness instead of his knowledge and ability. Also, true-false tests do not necessarily measure the students' understanding of the principle.

True-false examples:

.........A.   Among the early Church membership could be found skilled workers in almost every trade.

.........B.   The original "Law of Consecration" as introduced in Missouri, was later followed in Utah.

.........C.   The first five presidents of the Church were close associates of the Prophet Joseph Smith.

..........D. Health was a problem for the missionaries who left Nauvoo to go on missions to England.

..........E. It is the service to be rendered, not the office held, that is important in the Church.

True-False with correction if false:

..........A. John Taylor was President of the Church when the manifesto was issued.   ....

..........B. The Church was organized in the year 1829.

....

V. MATCHING TYPE TESTS

There are two types of matching tests. The first is called **completion-matching.** In this type, an essential word or phrase is omitted from each sentence of a list. At the end of, or beside the list of sentences is a list of words or phrases which contain the best answer for each word omitted. The difference between this and the sentence-completion form is that in the completion-matching form there will be only one or two more answers than are needed, while in the sentence-completion form, there are four or five possible choices for each.

The second type of matching test is called **column-matching.** In this form, two columns of statements are placed side by side and the numbers of one column are matched with the numbers or letters of the other. Some of the characteristics of matching can be observed in the examples given below. The more obvious ones have to do with form. There should be more answers in Part II than are needed in Part I. This reduces the matter of chance to a minimum. Only one answer can be correct for each statement. It will help the student if the items in Part II are arranged alphabetically or logically. Great care should be taken to avoid having any clues in either part which would suggest the correct answer. An example would be if one statement and one answer used either a singular subject or verb, or if only one pair had a plural subject.

Advantages and disadvantages:

Among the **advantages** of using this form is the fact that many questions can be answered in a short space. This is because the same set of answers can be used for a large number of items. Take the Godhead for example, probably thirty or thirty-five questions could be devised to which the answer would be either the Father, the Son, or the Holy Ghost. Having several items use the same answer in this manner will reduce guessing to a minimum.

The greatest usefulness in this type of test comes in answering questions concerning *who, what, when* and *where.*

Whether or not it tests the more complicated mental processes, whether it makes the student think, depends upon its construction. By matching principles with illustrations of the principles in action, the student is called upon to discriminate, compare, and conclude. Such a procedure calls for the same sort of mental processes that are demanded when an individual is asked to give an original illustration of a principle he has learned. This type of short-answer test enables one to make a rapid survey of a particular phase of a subject.

The **disadvantages** are that matching tests are difficult to construct. It is so easy to leave undone the large variety of specifics which need to be heeded. Clues that one had not suspected, or more than one correct answer, are apt to appear most unexpectedly. Furthermore, it fits the simpler items so well, such as events and their dates, that more complicated (and often more useful) associations are apt to be neglected. Small units of subject matter rarely furnish the homogeneity demanded of a good matching test and hence a small unit of instruction is difficult to test adequately using this form.

Matching Test Examples: (completion type)

Part I	Part II
A. ( ) The reuniting of the body and the spirit is called......	1. Spirit Children.
	2. Adam and Eve became subject to death.
	3. Exaltation.
B. ( ) The Fall has to do with........................	4. Resurrection.
	5. Disembodied spirits.
C. ( ) In the pre-mortal stage of our existence we were....	6. Adam becoming mortal.
	7. Our sins, if we repent.
D. ( ) Christ, our Redeemer, atoned for.........................	
E. ( ) The effect of the Fall was that........	

Matching Test Examples: (columnar type)

Part II

( ) a. Joseph Smith
( ) b. Brigham Young
( ) c. Oliver Cowdery
( ) d. John Taylor
( ) e. Martin Harris

1. Converted a Campbelite minister.
2. Was with Joseph Smith at the time of the martyrdom.
3. President of the Quorum of Twelve at the time of the Prophet's death.
4. Was scribe in translating the Book of Mormon.
5. Ninth President of the Church.
6. Led an apostate group.
7. Mortgaged home in order that the Book of Mormon could be published.

VI. PROBLEM-SOLVING TESTS:

Problem-solving is probably the single most useful teaching and testing tool of all. This is because this form makes it obvious to both student and teacher whether or not the student can apply a principle to a real life situation. It takes the principle out of the realm of the abstract and puts it in a here-and-now situation which the student is facing or will face in the future. You may be more familiar with this form being called the "case history method," though case-history is more properly applied to an incident which has already occurred. Also, this form is similar to the essay-type, the difference being that in the problem-solving there may be many "right" answers. That is, there is seldom a problem which can be solved in only one way.

Whenever we place a student in a here-and-now situation, he is faced with the necessity of judging it and making a decision as to how to cope with it. For instance, which of the two following situations would you feel was more valuable to an explorer and would tell you the most about him

1. Teacher A asks the students to list the rules for applying First Aid in any given situation.

2. Teacher B asks the class to suppose that they are at the beach (or in the mountains) on an outing with a group their own age. Three of them leave the group and swim into a secluded cove out of sight and of earshot of the main group. In diving one of them strikes his head on a rock and does not come back to the surface. The other two are able to find him and pull him from the water. His head is bleeding profusely and they are not sure whether or not he is breathing. List the first five things you would do.

This method may take more time and more imagination than other testing forms, but the result will be infinitely more valuable to both students and teacher.

Advantages and Disadvantages:

The **advantages** of problem-solving tests are: more telling results; no discipline problem, because of the student's sustained interest; and more accuracy in measuring the ability to apply learned principles than any other method.

Its **disadvantages** lie mostly in careless construction and presentation of problems, or poorly chosen problems. Unless the problem is one which truly represents a real life possibility, there will be little interest on the part of the student, regardless of his age. This does not mean that you cannot use problems which were faced in the past, such as situations by which the pioneers were confronted. But to use this type of problem you need to be sure that the principle involved is applicable to today's living.

Care must be taken not to structure the problem so that one factual sentence will give the answer. In other words, give them enough material to direct their thinking in the search, but not enough to actually give them a solution. A further disadvantage is the ease with which the student can go off on a tangent unless you provide constant guidance.

EXAMPLES: Since two examples have already been included, that should be sufficient to get your own imagination working. Make them real here-and-now situations and make them fit whatever principles you are teaching.

Now that we have had a glimpse of the variety of test that can be used in Church classes (and which you can construct to fit your own particular group), it is hoped all of us will do far more evaluating than before. To those of you who have done none at all, we hope you will now see the value of tests to both you and your students.

AND WHAT ABOUT YOU?

One final thought, in all this evaluating Don't Forget You! Most of this testing is done to see how effective your teaching **has been.** But all of us need a checklist of our own long before we start testing others. Try answering the following questions, then check your progress by answering them again every six months:

1. How is my gospel scholarship? Do I have a definite study program for continually adding to my knowledge?
2. How is my attitude? Am I truly committed to the gospel? To the program of the Church?
3. Do I have a fervent testimony not only of the gospel, but of the importance of my particular job in it?
4. Have I made a special effort to understand the age group that I teach? And the individuals in my class?
5. Have I made a special effort to learn something of the methods and techniques of teaching? Do I use a variety of teaching methods?
6. Do I **cheerfully** participate in **all** of the Ward and Stake meetings which are required of one in my position?
7. Am I committed to the enlistment program of my organization?
8. Am I really satisfied that I am trying to set the best possible example in my living of the gospel?

POINTS TO REMEMBER:

1. Testing, evaluating tests, and keeping records of the results is the best way to understand the progress of your students and therefore the effectiveness of your teaching.
2. Self-evaluation is needed throughout life, so we must teach students how to analyze themselves and how to accept evaluation from others.
3. We "measure" knowledge and "evaluate" ability.
4. There are five basic steps in evaluation that we should learn and use:
   A. State objectives clearly.
   B. Define general objectives in terms of student behavior.
   C. Devise problem-solving situations which will reveal the desired behavior and thinking.

    D. Keep a record of student behavior.

    E. Interpret the recorded behavior in the light of your objectives.

5. There are many types of simple tests which can be constructed by almost any teacher. However, problem-solving, because of student involvement is the most effective means of evaluating the *whole* student.

6. Though testing our students automatically evaluates our own performance, we also need to analyze ourselves regularly with a list of pertinent questions about our attitudes, our convictions, and our techniques and teaching methods.

CHAPTER XII

All This and Be a Shepherd Too

"If thou lovest me, feed my lambs."[1] Thus spoke the Saviour to all who would follow Him in teaching the gospel. Now that we have talked about the technical side of teaching, we come back to His words. Though we try to learn all we can of the basic principles of education that we might be more effective teachers, our most fundamental premise remains to love His children whom we teach. In gospel classes, the most effective teacher is not the one with the most technical knowledge of education. Instead, he is the one who has the greatest love of God and His children, and who combines that love with all the technical knowledge he can acquire. Christ was

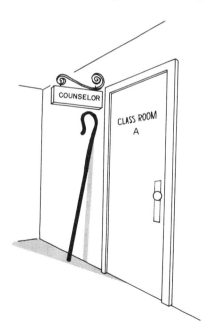

Fig. 81

the greatest teacher, not because He had all knowledge, but because He combined that knowledge with the greatest love.

THE ROLE OF SHEPHERD

Being a shepherd to those we teach infers such love. It infers guidance, giving of purpose and direction to the lives of the members of our class. We are, in effect, the counselors of God. We stand as earthly guides to a handful of His lambs, to do our part in bringing them safely back to Him. This is not done by coercion, we are not "sheep dogs nipping at their heels." They are free agents, but they are not born with knowledge of the plan of salvation and its importance in their lives. They need to be guided to this knowledge; counseled as to its application in today's world; helped to learn to make their own decisions on the basis of *spiritual* values instead of physical or material values.

This involves more than advice-giving — for advice-givers accomplish very little. Instead, it involves direction-giving, purpose-giving. We cannot, either as teachers or as parents, advise our children to eternal life; nor push them; nor do *for* them the things which must be done. We **can** show them the gospel and the results of gospel living in our own lives. We **can** give them assignments and problems to solve which will give them practice in thinking for themselves and making decisions on their own. We *can* help them analyze their own mistakes so they can grow strong and wise enough to make the right decisions in future situations. For instance, if you were working with teenagers and a social was being planned, you might know that a certain kind of music, refreshments, or decorations would not be really suitable for the occasion. But it still might be useful to let them try their way. Both of you might be surprised, and both of you might learn something valuable for future use. On the other hand, they should not be permitted to make decisions that would be contrary to the teachings of the Church, such as dancing past midnight at a Saturday night party in the Ward. Modesty in clothing, moral actions, and clean speech must be enforced whether it is their pleasure or not. Develop discernment as to where the line must be drawn to give them as much room for growth

¹John 21:26.

as possible and still not depart from Church standard and Church planned programs.

Nor does the shepherd forget his sheep once he leaves the corral, for often the best teaching is done outside the classroom: A moment or two in the hall or the parking lot; a casual meeting alone in which a boy or a girl might ask a question about a personal problem. A casual moment so that he can pretend it is a matter of small importance until he gets your reaction. If you show disapproval in voice or words or expression, a judgmental attitude, he will say no more but pass it off as inconsequential. And you may have lost forever the opportunity to be of value in that person's life.

Try to match his casualness, show friendly interest, and let him tell you about it in his own way: *listen.* Show him in every way you can that while you may despise a thing he has done, you love him as a person. This is a difficult thing to understand. Even many adults are unable to differentiate between the person and his act. As teachers we need to understand and to practice it constantly, so that others may see the principle in action. The Lord tells us that we may rebuke strongly when led to do so by the Holy Ghost; but that afterward we should show the person rebuked an extra amount of love, "lest he esteem thee to be his enemy."

To the shepherd of the lambs of God, counseling is a major part of his care of them. Counseling is defined as the process of assisting people successfully to understand and solve their everyday problems, to the end that they might achieve a satisfactory and happy-life adjustment. Or as Shirley A. Hemrin put it, "Guidance is helping John to see through himself in order that he may see himself through."

SOME BASIC PRINCIPLES OF COUNSELING

Briefly then, let us look at some of the principles generally held to be fundamental in the counseling of students.

1. **Guidance is concerned with the individual as a group member.** When a teacher ceases to think in terms of aiding individuals, it is doubtful that his work should be called "guidance."

Fig. 82

Guidance is concerned with the Individual as a Group Member

However, in working with the individual, the counselor must not overlook the fact that the individual functions always in a social setting and as a member of groups. Therefore, the counselor considers the contemporary social setting and the social demands imposed upon individuals. He considers himself responsible not only for counseling particular students, but for helping them to gain group experiences needed to increase their self-understanding through increased understanding of others, further he helps them to learn how to establish and maintain good personal relationships.

2. **Guidance is concerned with the whole student.** The counselor knows that he cannot advise a student regarding his choice of vocation, for instance, apart from consideration of his personality, educational achievement, strong interest, health, and the like.

Fig. 83   *Our concern is with the "Whole Student"*

Fig. 84   *Guidance implies Counsel, not Compulsion*

3. **Guidance implies counsel, not compulsion.** Compulsion is too often used when guidance could be employed. More frequently than some counselors care to admit, a student's "poor choice" does not turn out to be so poor as the counselor expected. Even if it does prove to be a poor one, the student may gain more than he loses by the experience. To achieve optimum personality development, each of us needs to experience a fair share of both success and failure. Hence, to deprive a student of his right to make a bad decision may hamper him in his growing up.

Fig. 85

Guidance is a Gradual and Continuous Process

4. **Guidance is a gradual and continuous process.** Too often teachers and counselors attempt to achieve the guidance objective through a single act or a short period of concentrated action. This shows a lack of understanding about guidance being a process, not an act. It is true that much useful information can be obtained about students during a short intensive

period of analytical and diagnostic work at the time of a student's entry into the class. However, more, and more valuable, information may be obtained by studying the student continuously through the year or years.

Fig. 86
Students should be helped to make their own decision

5. **Guidance is directed toward helping the student to become progressively more able to help himself.** When a student is encouraged and permitted to make choices and decisions, when he is aided in doing this by being permitted to share (as far as possible) in the study of his strengths and weaknesses, he has a much better chance of becoming progressively more able to help himself, than he does when most of his important choices and decisions are made for him by parents, teachers, and other adults.

TEACH HIM TO STAND ALONE WITH THE LORD
Each individual must learn to stand alone with the Lord. He will never be a free agent as long as he leans too heavily

on others in making the decisions which affect his life. Teach him to be humble enough to depend on the Lord, and strong enough to stand alone. Brigham Young said:

> "Now those men, or those women, who know no more about the power of God, and the influences of the Holy Spirit, than to be led entirely by another person, suspending their own understanding, and pinning their faith upon another's sleeve, will never be capable of entering into celestial glory. . . . They cannot rule themselves, to say nothing of ruling others, but they must be dictated to in every trifle, like a child. They cannot control themselves in the least, but James, Peter, or somebody else must control them. . . . They can never hold sceptres of glory, majesty, and power in the celestial kingdom. Who will? Those who are valiant and inspired with the true independence of heaven, who will go forth boldly in the service of their God, leaving others to do as they please, determined to do right, though all mankind besides should take the opposite course. Will this apply to any of you? Your own hearts can answer."[2]

GIVE HIM A SENSE OF DESTINY

It has been said that in the divine blueprint, each of us has a place which no one else can fill; that if we do not fill it, it will remain a blank space. To the Latter-day Saint, this means that in the Plan of Salvation each child of God has his part to play. In so far as we fail, the plan will be incomplete, less than perfect.

This sense of destiny was the source of the dedication of our pioneer ancestors. The conviction that they had been entrusted with opening and carrying forth the Last Great Dispensation of the gospel plan, gave them at once a sense of challenge and of fulfillment. It gave them the courage and the stamina to withstand hunger and cold and persecution. To them, theirs was a high and sacred calling which lifted their spirits to such heights that physical and material things

---

[2]*Journal of Discourses,* Vol. 1, page 312.

Fig. 87

Give them a Sense of Destiny

did not matter enough to stop them from giving their all in fulfilling that destiny.

Our sense of destiny, our challenge, is the same today. The material problems may be updated to the nuclear-space age, but the basic human problems remain the same for each generation: Will we strive to keep the commandments of God, not for His benefit but for our own? Will we stand firm when confronted with hardship and persecution (social pressure)? Will the faith of our generation withstand the adulation of the world, the moral weakness of many of the people around us, and the weakening influences of too much material wealth too easily gained?

These are the questions each generation must ask of itself as it seeks to verify its faith in God and to understand the Plan of Salvation. This is the sense of destiny each teacher must find for himself, that he may guide those he teaches to the same goal. In our classes, Church History must be studied not as facts to be memorized, but as a direction-giver, a purpose-giver to help our students to understand and accept their share in the completion of the Divine Plan. Only when they become personally involved will they gain the conviction, the testimony, necessary to make them **want** to dedicate their lives to the fruition of that plan. Then as Jesus said, when they have lost their lives in service to the children of God, they will find eternal life. "This is my work and my glory to bring to pass the immortality and eternal life of man."[3]

Could you and I find a greater challenge, a more satisfying service than to guide our students to this sense of destiny, each for himself?

Now as we come to the end of this book we find that, in a sense, only YOU can write "The End." As a wise man once said, "Knowledge has no value unless it is used." Only if YOU use the principles in this book, use them to help you to become a more effective teacher, only then will this book be of value to you. Only then will its purpose be achieved. For only then will you understand that YOU TOO CAN TEACH!

[3]Moses 1:39, Pearl of Great Price.

INDEX